Platinum Publishing

Co-Founder of Sherwood Mortgage Group
ATHENA CONSTANTINOU

#mortgagedonts

STOP UNNECESSARY EXPENSES, STRESS AND
ANXIETY WHEN SETTING UP YOUR MORTGAGE

Platinum Publishing
c/o Fatima Omar Khamissa
18-3555 Don Mills Road
Suite 131
Toronto
Ontario
M2H 3N3

Like anything in life, there are no guarantees that using the methods mentioned by the publisher of by any of the contributors will result in the same success mentioned.

Although the author and publisher have made every effort to ensure that the information in this book was correct at press time, the author and publisher do not assume and hereby disclaim any liability to any party for any loss, damage, or disruption caused by errors or omissions, whether such errors or omissions result from negligence, accident, or any other cause.

The information contained within this book is strictly for educational purposes. If you wish to apply ideas contained in this book, you are taking full responsibility for your actions

Typesetting and formatting by access ideas

ISBN: 978-0-9953136-4-4

Table of Contents

An Ounce of Prevention

If a magical fairy had given me a dollar for all the #mortgagedonts I've come across in my career, I'd be rich. #mortgagedonts are what I've labelled seemingly insignificant behaviours that cause huge mortgage problems. These problems result in added expenses, increased anxiety and sky high stress levels. All of which are undesirable consequences of a situation that is more often than not, totally preventable.

Writing #mortgagedonts was an idea that popped up in conversation one day as a colleague and I were discussing our problem files and I realized that almost all of them were preventable. My initial intent was to start a twitter series with a weekly #mortgagedonts tip to point out a specific challenging behaviour. As I started writing down some of my recent experiences, I noticed that all the problems could be lumped into certain groups which I thought were worth sharing with a larger audience.

The one obvious thing you'll notice in this book is that I don't talk about fraud or criminal activity. It's an assumed fact that these behaviours are never tolerated so I don't give these topics any attention. Same goes for rates, pricing and market analyses. I don't mention any of that in this book because I'm not interested in discussing the mortgage industry from an economics perspective. My focus is to show you that there's a behaviour aspect to obtaining a mortgage, and as humans, we're prone to making mistakes. These mistakes are costly – both in the form of time and money. They lead to high stress situations that almost 90% of the time, could have been prevented. My goal is to not only show you where the errors are made, but offer suggestions as to how to prevent them for your own mortgage (should you ever find yourself in a similar situation).

The book's sections can be read independently or straight through in order. If you're reading in sections I would recommend starting with chapter 1 and 2 so you get a little background of how every application starts. There are also 5 unicorn stories which are sprinkled throughout the book and they're written in *italics* so they stand out. These stories (much like the rare and mythical creature they're named after), don't happen often, if ever. I added them in as a reality check for those going through little bumps along their financing road. They're all true stories and they're meant to put things into perspective as to how quickly minor issues can escalate into ugly situations.

The fact is that mortgages blow up before closing dates. Think of a blow up as a denied approval. Imagine purchasing a plane ticket, getting to the terminal and preparing to check in your bags. You're talking and laughing with your friends about the deal of a vacation you got when suddenly, the airline rep interrupts you. She can't print your boarding pass because your passport expired. The same concept applies to a mortgage blow up. You were given an approval but you can't close the transaction because you're missing or unable to satisfy a lender condition. Some files blow up on a larger scale than others and unfortunately, it really is more common than we'd like it to be. It's every borrower's nightmare when it happens and every mortgage professional's angst to try to work through and provide alternate solutions on an extremely tight timeline.

One can argue that it's the mortgage agent's fault for failing to ask for the right information up front. A client in these situations will say 'but you never asked me' or 'you never told me'. They will believe that the mortgage professional didn't do their job thoroughly. Others, believe that the fault lies with the clients who should be more forthcoming and accurate with their personal details. Regardless of which camp you're in, a blow up involves everyone. So rather than try to point fingers and lay blame, I've put together some thoughts that may help everyone involved in the mortgage financing transaction so that blow ups can become a thing of the past.

Chapter 1

I Can't Draw a Stick Figure to Save My Life, But It May Help With Yours

The word mortgage sparks different reactions for different people. For most, it's a daunting task of collecting paperwork, jumping through lender hoops and having to prove their worthiness to borrow the money they need to get into their starter home. The anxiety kicks in and you're wondering if your credit is good enough, your income high enough and if the mortgage gods are going to grant you an approval. For others, the word mortgage evokes a sense of confusion. It strikes a fear deep within their soul, and their eyes glaze as I speak to them. All they want to do is purchase their condo and do the fun things like pick out paint and furniture. They don't understand what a mortgage is other than knowing they need one and these clients really need hand-holding. And finally, there's a tiny group of people who hear the word mortgage and feel a sense of accomplishment. It's a step towards proving that they've made it! They have enough savings, make enough money, and are responsible enough to make the monthly payment. It's almost like reaching a milestone...You finally made it to adulthood!

Just over 20 years ago I interviewed for a position as a mortgage specialist assistant at a big bank. I remember one of the questions they asked me was: 'do you know what a mortgage is?', to which I responded: 'No'. The gentleman, who later became my boss, looked at me, laughed and said 'it's just a fancy word for a loan for a house'. That's bizarre, I thought to myself. 'Since loans for students are student loans, loans for cars are car loans and loans for RRSP's are RRSP loans, why don't we just call it a house or home loan?' I asked. He shrugged his shoulders, chuckled and said 'that's a good question. I have no idea.'

According to the Oxford Dictionary:

Mortgage (noun), is "A legal agreement by which a bank, building society, etc. lends money at interest in exchange for taking title of the debtor's property, with the condition that the conveyance of title becomes void upon the payment of the debt." Its origins are late Middle English and old French, meaning 'dead pledge'. Mort is Latin for dead (mortuus) + gage which means 'pledge'.

If we take a look back in history, we'll see some fun facts on how mortgage loans have evolved through the years. (Source: FSCO website)

- *Taking on a mortgage is the most common way Ontarians can get a piece of the housing market – and has been for a long time. The mortgage industry dates back hundreds of years. But while the purpose of these loans has stayed the same, they've evolved from a simple repayment plan to a much more complex financial transaction.*

- *Mortgages originated in England when people did not have the resources to purchase land in one transaction. Buyers would get loans directly from the seller – no banks or outside parties were involved. Unlike today, purchasers were not able to live on the land until the entire amount was paid. And, if they failed to keep up with payments, they would forfeit their right to the land as well as any prior payments they made to the seller.*

- *By the 1900s most mortgages involved long-term loans where only monthly interest was paid while the borrower saved towards repayment of the original sum. Major world events, like the Great Depression of the 1920s and the two World Wars however, led to many borrowers being unable to repay even the interest on a property that was often now worth less than their original loan, and many lenders carrying a loan that was not secured by the value of the property. This resulted in the introduction of long-term fully amortized mortgages that repaid some of the principal and some of the interest each month in a payment that was fixed for upwards of 25 years.*

- *The Canada Mortgage and Housing Corporation (CMHC) was created in 1946 to administer the National Housing Act and today sells mandatory mortgage loan insurance when the buyer is putting less than 20 per cent down on the price of their new home. Mortgage loan insurance compensates lenders when borrowers default on their mortgage loans.*

- *The rise of inflation in the 1970s altered mortgages into the products we know now. As interest rates climbed, lenders and borrowers found themselves locked into fully amortized loans that didn't reflect interest rate changes. The creation of the partially amortized mortgage, which protects both lenders and borrowers from fluctuations in the market, mean that instead of 20- to 30-year terms, one, three or five-year terms amortized across 20 to 25 years have become a better option. Partially amortized mortgages are now one of the most common mortgage types in Canada.*

- *Making the down payment for a mortgage easier to attain, the Home Buyer's Plan, which allows Canadians to withdraw money from their Registered Retirement Savings Plans (RRSPs) on a tax-free basis to buy a home, was introduced by the Canadian government in 1992.*

- *On July 1, 2008, under the Mortgage Brokerages, Lenders and Administrators Act, 2006 [New Window], the Government of Ontario has required all businesses and individuals who conduct mortgage brokering activities in the province to be licensed with the Financial Services Commission of Ontario (FSCO). Mortgage brokers and agents play a big role in the mortgage process, with 51 per cent of first-time home buyers using their services according to a 2016 CMHC survey. Under the Act, all mortgage brokers and agents need to meet specific education, experience, and suitability requirements with the goal of increased consumer protection, competition and professionalism in the industry.*

- *Mortgages have evolved from repayments that provided protection and benefits only for the landowner, to a system in which both the borrower and the lender can enter into the transaction with confidence.* (Source: Fsco website)

I started working in February 1999 and since then I have matched thousands of borrowers to lenders. Although I didn't know the word prior to this date, mortgages are all I've dealt with since I graduated university. I was trained to be a specialist; not a generalist learning a little about many products. I learned A LOT about mortgages, and only mortgages, and as a result, have become an expert in putting the pieces together to get you home. Not only is it my job to look out for you as the borrower but I also have to ensure that my lenders get the right borrowers for their products. The more accurate I submit your file, the more efficient the process is and the easier your file funds.

Since I've started this career path, I've helped borrowers in endless types of situations because I think in stories. Some people think in shapes. Others think in numbers. Some see colours and patterns. For me, it's always about the story and a mortgage is just a more complicated story. Actually, let me correct that. A mortgage is a risk based, complicated story where the main characters (you), know the ending (for example, refinancing to pay out debt), and it's the middle we have to figure out: how do we got to your desired goal. As a rookie mortgage specialist, in order to capture as many details from my clients during meetings, I started doodling as they spoke. Stick figures with arrows to houses meant a purchase. Circular motions with dollar signs attached to it would sometimes mean income. Big circles with the word 'credit' written in the middle and a diagonal slash slicing through would mean credit challenges or issues. My drawings not only prompted me to remember the details to each client's situation, but they also helped my customers understand a sometimes complicated process.

It never failed that after every initial meeting I got asked for a copy of the doodles. 20 years later, I'm still drawing and they're still taking a copy of it home. It's hard to learn the language of mortgage and remember all the details we discussed over a half hour period. It's not so hard to follow the road map of stick figures and universal symbols. My doodles have helped plenty of first time buyers take on the big, scary world of home financing.

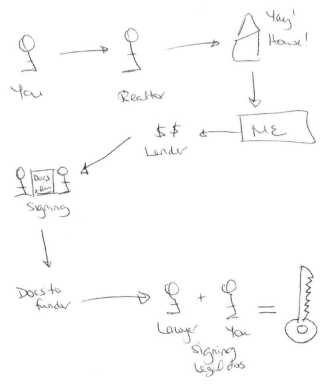

Figure A: Process of a purchase file

The reality is that mortgages aren't so big and scary and the process is quite simple. The industry today consists of a few key players:

1. Client/applicant/borrower – this is you because you have a need to finance a property. You now have the option of approaching one of two mortgage originators:

2. Bank mortgage originator: This is a bank employee who will gather your information to see if you qualify for that specific bank's mortgage. Sometimes they're branch employees and sometimes they're a specialized sales force with the sole purpose of putting together mortgages for approval and funding.

3. Mortgage Agent/Broker: This is a licensed (and usually self-employed) individual who also collects your information to see what you qualify for. They have many lender partners and are not limited to only one solution. They too, prepare your file for approval and funding.

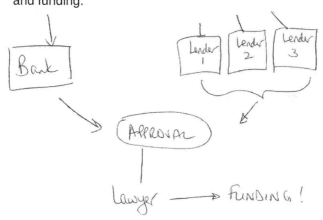

Figure B – Home financing Key Players

As you can see, most of the process is fairly similar except in one area: your choice of service provider at the mortgage origination stage. It's this very crucial stage which dictates your client experience. Although there are good and bad bank employees, and good and bad mortgage agent/brokers, the most fundamental difference between them is that a mortgage agent/broker works for YOU and not one specific lender. Mortgage agent/brokers have full reign on placing your deal with the lender of best fit so you get the best pricing and features for you.

The reason I wrote this book is because mortgages have so many aspects to them from bond market yields and economic trends to market analysis and servicing. For the purpose of this book, I'm not interested in any of these. I want to identify common errors and pitfalls during the mortgage application process so that you can prevent them from happening to you. Your home buying or refinancing should be a seamless and stress free experience and each chapter is set up to help in a similar format:

1. A description of a mortgage characteristic and its relevance

2. A purchase and a refinance common error in the form of a true story (all names and identifying factors have been changed to protect identities)

3. Doodle drawing(s)

4. Impact of the error on the mortgage process

5. Explanation of how to avoid these errors during your application

Ideally, these suggestions will prevent having your financing cancelled last minute because of a misunderstanding of a key fact. It'll prevent extra costs ranging from real estate delays and extra legal fees, to movers being put on hold or delayed debt payouts that could impact your credit score.

Although there are many errors and oversights that could happen during the mortgage process, this book focuses on the most common ones I've seen repeatedly over the last 20 years. The ones which tend to cause unnecessary grief and anxiety because for the most part, they're preventable.

The first step to simplifying home financing is to forget the 'one size fits all' model of mortgages that we've grown accustomed to in the last couple of decades. With all the government regulatory changes that have occurred in the last few years, mortgages have become more personalized. Just because you buy a home or need to refinance, doesn't mean you get the same mortgage your friends did. Now, more than ever, you need a mortgage professional to guide you. Lenders are coming out with more and more niche products targeted to specific types of borrowers so you need the guidance of an industry professional to help get you the best options. As a consumer, it'll be a huge benefit to have a relationship with a mortgage agent/broker because it will grant you access to innovative lenders with new products and offerings.

For those who don't speak mortgage, here's a simple breakdown of the different types of mortgage products out there and why you would need them:

Purchase – Self-explanatory. You want to buy a property and you don't have enough savings to pay for the whole thing on your own. You set up this type of financing to kick in the difference of funds that you haven't saved yet. The condo price is $500,000 and you have $100,000 for downpayment so the mortgage applied for would be for $400,000.

Purchase mortgages fall into 2 categories: Conventional and high ratio. A conventional mortgage is arranged for those who have a minimum 20% downpayment and results in not being charged a mortgage insurance premium. A high ratio mortgage is a purchase with less than 20% downpayment. These buyers pay a one-time high ratio insurance premium (insured through CMHC, Genworth or Canada Guaranty), to access lower downpayment products.

Refinance – you already own the house and want to take out some equity for a specific use. In other words, you're using your house as your bank. Let's say your house is worth $650,000 and your outstanding mortgage balance is $210,000. You'd like to finish your basement and update the sea foam coloured cabinets which is going to cost you about $80,000. Based on today's lending guidelines, the maximum mortgage you can apply for is 80% of your home's value: $650,000 x 80% = $520,000

When you add your current mortgage of $210,000 + the $80,000 you need, your application would be for a new mortgage of $290,000. Well within the allowable limit.

Renewal – You own the property and your mortgage term is now coming to an end. At this time, you should be calling up your mortgage advisor to seek out information on what current rates look like. Are you eligible for a no-fee switch to another lender who has more competitive rates than the ones your current lender is offering?

Equity lines of credit – Sometimes these get set up to buy a property and sometimes they get added on to a property that you already own. They help with cash flow because you only pay interest on the money you've used. They're also re-advanceable so if you've paid off some of the balance, you can reuse them again (should you need to).

Construction mortgage – This too, is pretty self-explanatory. You want to build your home but don't have enough funds. The challenge here is that we have a property that won't have its full value until it's 100% complete. These types of mortgages fund in draws so you keep building in stages. The entire amount of the mortgage is dispersed once you reach 100% complete and have the appropriate occupancy permits.

Now that you've had your crash course in mortgage types, let's review 5 factors involved in mortgage risk assessment. My business partner lovingly calls these the 5 C's of credit, and drills them in to every new hire who joins our team:

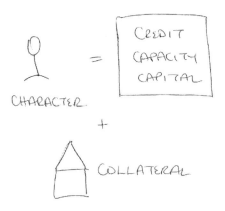

Figure C – The 5 C's of Credit

A lender reviews your overall **CHARACTER** as a borrower and this character consists of 3 other C's:

CREDIT – your repayment history and habits and is reflected as a beacon score on your credit bureau

CAPACITY – your ability to make the payments

CAPITAL – your portion of ownership in the property – either via the downpayment if you're purchasing, or the equity if you already own it

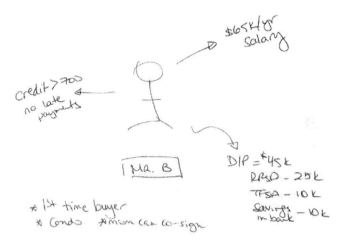

Figure D - Character profiling of a borrower in an initial conversation. In this case, parent was available to co-sign if he didn't qualify on his own.

Usually, one of the factors in an applicant's character assessment will dictate the route the application will take. It's imperative that during this initial getting to know each other phase, we're honest and open about everything. Once the lender gets a good idea of who you are as a borrower, they'll look at the final C which is **COLLATERAL**: the property you're looking to buy or refinance. It's understandable that the type, condition and location of the property would be assessed. This allows the lender to determine the marketability of the real estate should you stop paying the mortgage and they have to recoup their funds.

Throughout this book, it'll be this information gathering part of the application process that I'll be addressing. If it's incomplete or done incorrectly, it will negatively impact your financing. Asking questions and getting answers seems like an easy enough task so how, do you ask, can it go wrong?

Errors are sometimes due, but not limited to:

a. A lack of knowledge on the part of the applicant. You don't know what information I need so you don't volunteer it and this is usually due to…..

b. The mortgage professional not asking the right questions or not requesting the correct documents. If I don't listen to your answers and probe further for clarification, I can't blame you for forgetting to tell me that you pay $1700/month in child support (which is a vital fact I need to know).

c. Fear of disclosing too much. This tends to arise from a lack of trust and comfort level with your mortgage professional. Information is purposely withheld because a borrower is afraid of saying too much and possibly being punished. Although I may be asking you all the right questions, if you withhold a key fact because you feel it's none of my business, I won't be able to accurately present your situation to the lender.

d. Embarrassment or the fear that you're the only one in 'this situation'. You're embarrassed to admit past mistakes because you think we haven't seen your type of situation before and will judge you. I can honestly tell you that we've probably seen it and dealt with it many times and we're definitely not judging. The only thing we're thinking about is how we're going to get you to your desired result.

Other issues include the belief that you, the applicant, shouldn't have to disclose much information or have to provide all the documents I've requested. I understand that digging up your last two years' tax returns is time consuming, but wouldn't you rather get an approval for a longer mortgage term with a competitive rate, over a shorter term with a higher rate and lender fee? Sometimes, it's those added schedules in that tax return that push you from one solution into a better one.

And finally, another common obstacle I see which leads to frustration, is the idea that an applicant is entitled to financing. Usually these clients have one of their 5 C's extremely strong. A high income earner feels she should get an 'A' deal because she more than qualifies for the mortgage. She has sloppy credit history and all her credit cards are operating at limit. The borrower with a ton of equity in his house feels that he shouldn't have to income qualify because there's no way he's going to let the bank have his house. He'll move mountains to make sure the monthly payment is on time. He currently has no job or income and living off his savings. Last time I checked though, once the savings run out, you can't use your bricks to make the monthly payments. Just because an applicant has ONE exceptionally strong 'C', doesn't mean they automatically get approved for the best priced mortgage. There are niche products for these borrowers and they tend to have higher pricing because of the lack of/weaker other C's. Although these clients have one strong 'C', all their other 'C's' tend to be less than optimal which now makes them riskier borrowers. The more C's you're stronger on, the better your rate and mortgage will be.

Now that you have a better idea of what I do on a day-to-day basis let's get started on a quest through the land of mortgages. Think of me as the catalyst character; the one who solves the financing puzzle because my passion lies in helping the overwhelmed borrower. I help the ones who are downright petrified of the word mortgage, to the well versed professionals who have owned many properties and are overwhelmed with their busy lives so they're happy to have me orchestrate their financing. I've had a lot of success helping borrowers with simple stories as well as borrowers with complicated situations so I'm hoping that by following my suggestions, you too will realize that mortgages really are very simplistic in nature. You'll see that it's not like learning a new complicated and intimidating language but more like solving a jigsaw puzzle. We have to make sure the right pieces are in the box so we can complete the whole picture.

Chapter 2

How to Find a Mortgage Broker

Want to buy a house? You may need money because you haven't saved enough to buy it outright. You went on a shopping bender by renovating your house and designing it so it was instagram-worthy and now you want to consolidate your debt? You need money out of your home equity to pay it all off. You want to buy your dream cottage by that pristine lake or an investment property to fund your retirement years? You need to hand over money so the place becomes yours.

How do you get started?

Some people walk into their local bank branch. Others ask google for the best mortgage brokerage and Sherwood Mortgage Group pops up. The rest? They either ask a friend, relative or realtor for a referral, and they'll send you over to their trusted professional, much like the example below:

You decide you want to buy your own place and you reach out to your friend to ask if they have a real estate agent they know and trust. "Of course I know a realtor!" says your friend and introduces you to the agent who helped her buy her place. The real estate agent is super professional and patient with you as he explains the home buying process. He's quite happy to take you shopping for your new condo. However, before he sends you listings and takes you out to see places, he needs a budget and a pre-approval from you. A budget? How are you supposed to know what you qualify for? All you know is that 1+ den condos in the area you want to move to, are $480,000. You have $20,000 that you've saved up for downpayment and you want your monthly carrying cost to be no more than $2000 all in. The realtor insists that he can't take you out to look at the building you want (and rightfully so), until you come back to him with a figure. You mention that you'll make an appointment with your branch to get a pre-approval. It's usually at this point that an experienced realtor will also recommend a mortgage agent/broker for a second opinion. Many times, the realtor or your friends/co-workers have gone through this process before you and will be happy to refer someone they've had a great experience working with.

You reach out to the mortgage professional because it makes sense that you should deal with someone who has access to many lenders. No one has prepared you up to this point but get ready to air out all your personal info and tell your story, which may go something along the lines of this other example:

Your landlord just gave you 60 days' notice that she's selling the condo you live in and moving to the US. Before putting it on the market, she's approached you to see if you're interested in buying it. You entertain the idea because you'd prefer to stay rather than move and find a new place. You doubt you have enough savings for a downpayment because you've spent so many years studying to become a lawyer. You're up to your eyeballs in student loan payments so although you're making good money, you're not even sure you would qualify for a mortgage based on your debt. You're very concerned, wondering if you have to pack up and move to another rental or if there's a chance you can buy this condo. What will that entail and will you be able to afford it without eating canned tuna for dinner every night the first year?

This is where our relationship begins. You have a challenge which requires money as the solution and I can help. I listen as you speak, ask a few questions and because I always have a pen nearby (paper not required as napkins also work), draw my stick figure sketches.

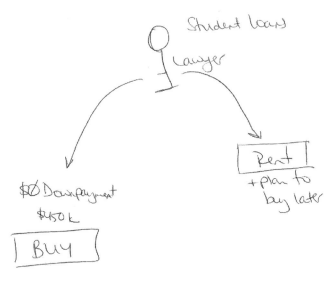

Figure E - Initial conversation doodle

I contemplate your story by envisioning possible solutions. My doodles get etched in my memory so every time I have to recall a detail of your file, I think of your stick figures. While my brain is processing and running different scenarios for solutions (think of playing Tetris when you could see the next piece that was going to fall and where you would place it), I'm sending you a summary email with:

1. A link to our online application portal where you can provide me your basic information and consent to pull your credit bureau

2. A list of documents I need you to send in - which will help me be as accurate as possible with my advice

3. My contact info with all the ways you can reach me

Upon completion of these steps I start reviewing the 5c's of your story and come up with the magic number your realtor wants: your maximum purchase price. The conversation between you and I is then going to head in one of two directions:

A. If the price I give you is more than you wanted, you're pleased. You know you can comfortably purchase in your target range. I'll set out your approximate monthly budget as well as list any additional documents and lender conditions that you would need to satisfy once you buy.

B. If the maximum price I give you is below what you were looking for, then we have a chat about how we get you into your dream property. There are a few solutions we discuss to see which one is more feasible for you. You go out looking for your place armed with all the info you need and the comfort level of knowing what you can afford. Again, like option A above, I'll provide you with a budget and a list of outstanding items.

If you already own your home though and you're looking for a refinance because you need to consolidate debt, the process is similar but not quite the same. You're still looking for someone to help you but instead of getting a referral from your realtor, you may go back to your current lender to ask for advice. Or, you may ask your friends and family for someone they know. Once we're connected, the process is similar. We discuss your challenge but in this case, it's not to find your maximum purchase price. You want to know how we can withdraw some of your equity to pay off debt (which is at a much higher interest rate). The application process is the same. I draw a doodle, you send me documents, and once again, I use your story to come up with the best solution for you. The end result here isn't a set of keys to a new home but a monthly cash flow reduction where we bring all your debt into one lower and manageable total monthly payment. Maybe you can use the extra funds you were dishing out in interest payments towards topping up your RRSP or TFSA. Maybe you can finally save up and go on that vacation you've been dreaming about. Or maybe, you can stop working that second job you picked up to make those minimum interest payments to begin with.

Finally, what if you don't need any money because your mortgage is coming up for renewal? I can still help by offering to shop around to see if I can get you a better rate for your new term. You're not sourcing money to achieve a goal in this scenario. You're sourcing money to find an overall interest cost savings. If you're in the market for a mortgage renewal, it'll come up in conversations with friends or family and someone is bound to say "I have someone who can help you!" With a quick phone call and a few questions, you should be able to get a rate with which you can make a decision on whether to switch your mortgage to a new lender.

Regardless of the type of transaction you need or which mortgage professional you work with, the communication process should always be a two way street. Although we need a lot of information from you to help you out, don't be shy or timid because you don't speak the language of mortgage. You as the consumer should be asking all the questions you want and getting informed. Most of your questions will be specific to your file however here are some general helpful questions you should be asking your mortgage professional (another list is provided in the appendix section):

1. If you can't approve my mortgage, will you have a plan B? Or will you just tell me I'm declined and I have to start this process all over again with someone else?

    - This is key for you to know because if you're on a time restriction, you may want to work with someone who already knows what plan B is.

2. How long does the approval process take?

    - Some lenders offer niche products or special rates and their turnaround will be slower than others because of the sheer volume of applications that get sent to them. Other lenders review your documentation with your application and this too, could take longer than a standard approval timeframe. Depending on your situation and the lender being considered, your mortgage specialist should be able to give you an idea of how long the process will take.

3. What documentation can I prepare for you?

    - Be wary of a mortgage professional who says they don't need any paperwork from you and they'll collect it once they have an approval. There's so much room for error that I highly recommend for you to provide your documentation up front with your application. By giving me your documents when we first start, I use exact figures and data as opposed to estimates and ballpark figures. More often than not, a borderline file that gives documents post-approval tends to have issues closer to the closing date. By having the data during the underwriting phase, I can get an approval for that same borderline deal with all conditions signed off and reduce my chances of problems during the closing.

4. What costs are going to be involved with this mortgage?

- Every mortgage has a cost involved to set it up. An 'A' mortgage has certain costs. An alternate mortgage has other costs. And private mortgages have their own set of costs. There's no reason why your mortgage professional shouldn't be able to give you an estimate of what you'll have to pay once they've secured an approval for you.

5. What type of mortgage are you putting together for me?

- Sometimes the only solutions available for you aren't worth the time and costs involved. If I'm re-financing your mortgage and putting you in a worse position than what you're starting with, I won't pursue it any further. Usually in situations where there are credit or income limitations we do our best to always provide an option that has at least one benefit for you. I should be able to show you this benefit and quantify it so you can make a decision on whether or not you want to proceed.

I get asked by clients all the time if they can "ask a stupid question". When it comes to your financing, there is no stupid question. We're talking about a lot of money. If it's not set up properly or the way you wanted it, it's costly to correct and even more expensive in the long run if it's not the right solution for you. Take the time to ask all the questions you need and don't feel like you're bothering anyone.

Unicorn Story 1: Change is good. But not while trying to secure a mortgage.

Alex is a loving mother of 4 kids and her dream was to get them out of their 2 bedroom rental apartment and into their own home. Because of her financial situation she opted to buy a house with her mother 6 years ago. When they finally found 'the one', they were in love. It was close to both of their workplaces and the school was a short drive away. It had a 5-car parking pad and a swimming pool! Her kids were so excited and Granny was moving in with them! The mortgage closed on time and the move went through beautifully with Alex & mom finally becoming homeowners!

3 years later, things changed. Alex met Sam, a loving and hard-working gentleman who she immediately clicked with. After a year of dating, they decided to move in together. Sam, a first time buyer himself, had no funds for downpayment. He came to the table with a good income and could help support the payments for a slightly larger house. Alex's mom had changed jobs, and their current home was no longer convenient for her. Her commute had increased by 40 minutes each way, so she was looking for a place of her own closer to work. The signs pointed to the family having to sell their current house to move onto the next chapter of their lives. They weren't worried about selling their home. They were more worried about finding a home they liked in a neighbouring town which could accommodate the kids' schooling, their jobs and their budget. Their realtor referred them over to us and I got started on finding Alex and Sam's maximum purchase price.

Assumptions that were made:

1. They would be buying a house rather than a property with maintenance fees.

2. Alex would be selling her house for $550,000 which at that time, was a fair market value.

3. Her mortgage was only $130,000 with a $4,000 penalty which left them with ample

funds to payout debt. Alex had a car loan with a large monthly payment and 2 small credit cards. Both with less than $1000 in outstanding balances.

4. They would have at least 20% downpayment towards the new house

5. To maximize their purchasing power, we had to find a lender that:

   a. allowed a 30 year amortization

   b. Had a competitive interest rate (both Alex and Sam and credit scores over 680 so they were eligible for best rates)

   c. accepted child tax benefit as an income because Alex was collecting almost $2500/month for her kids in addition to her pay at work

Alex's house was listed on the market in early August to show off the pool and it's split level style living which was an entertainer's dream. Open house after open house, showing after showing, plenty of people came by, interested in the property and looking for more information. In the meantime, Alex and Sam decided they wanted to go out looking at properties. They were confident that her house would sell in no time and agreeable with the conditions of the pre-approval. They were given a budget of no more than $600,000 with the following stipulations:

1. 20% downpayment from their sale proceeds

2. all debts for both of them, to be paid to $0 (Sam had a few outstanding accounts and he was sure he would be able to pay them to $0 by the closing date)

3. Firm sale agreement for the house that was on the market

4. Accepted purchase agreement and listing for the new house

5. Income confirmation which in their case was an employment letter, recent paystub and the last 2 years t4 slips in order to use all their overtime since they were hourly paid employees

6. 3 months bank statements to confirm Alex's child tax benefit deposit

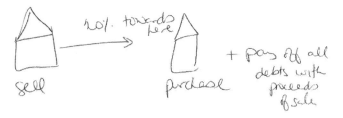

Figure F - Alex & Sam initial doodle

After seeing a few houses, they found it. A magnificent 5 bedroom house in Barrie, ON. They were moving to a larger city with ample schooling options and a 4-car garage. The backyard was perfect and the location would cut Sam's commute by 20 minutes. It would add 30 minutes to Alex's but she was fine with this if it meant her kids had access to the education they required. So, against the advice of myself and the realtor, Alex and Sam insisted on putting in a conditional offer. They couldn't risk losing this house. Their offer was accepted with a 5 day condition on financing and home inspection.

The realtor sent in the purchase agreement and listing. Alex and Sam sent in their income documents. The closing date was set to late November to give Alex and mom ample time to secure a strong offer on their home. We had 3 months within which to satisfy all the conditions but when I presented them an approval for their mortgage, issues started to surface.

"Is there any way we can go with 15% downpayment so I can hold on to some money for my kids' education?" asked Alex. A very wise request from a responsible parent, however a very different application that I now had to deal with. By reducing to a 15% downpayment, we would now be subject to high ratio mortgage rules which included a reduced 25 year amortization AND an insurance premium tacked on to a higher mortgage amount. I re-worked the numbers and determined that the deal still qualified. We double checked figures, went over net funds with the realtor and we all agreed to this new proposal. Well no sooner did we confirm this info and Sam calls me the next day to ask if he really has to pay out his debt. Once he realized that there were only 6 upcoming pay periods instead of the 7 (like he originally thought), he was concerned that he wouldn't have enough funds to pay everything out. Ideally, he wanted to leave one card unpaid.

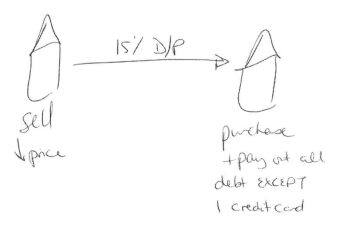

15% D/P

sell
↓ price

purchase
+pay ot all
debt EXCEPT
1 credit card

Figure G - Alex & Sam revised doodle

The realtor was getting frustrated that the financing condition hadn't been waived (it was day 4 of 5). We had an applicant who made more than half of her income as child tax credit (only accepted by a handful of lenders), a reduced downpayment and amortization, AND a request to not pay out debt. I requested a conference call with everyone. This constant changing of conditions after agreeing to them was going to stop. On the call, we discussed how we started off on one plan and were now heading towards a completely different mortgage solution that didn't qualify. Emotions ran high. Alex's house had now been on the market for almost 3 weeks with no offer. The concerns from everyone viewing the property was that it was on a main road with traffic and didn't have a garage. The realtor suggested a price drop from $550,000 to

$539,000. They agreed so one challenge was being dealt with.

I re-iterated the numbers with Alex, Sam and the realtor (on the call), so we would all be in agreement of the net proceeds. I confirmed what 15% downpayment plus closing costs would be in dollar figures and I ran the qualifying numbers without all the debt paid out. The mortgage didn't qualify. In order to proceed with this option, we would need a co-signor to add more income to the file. They both confirmed they didn't have one. Sam's parents were retired and still had a small mortgage on their home. Alex's mom was looking to get her own place. We were forced to continue with the debt payout and Sam agreed that if he fell short on the amount he needed, he would reach out to mom and dad for help with the difference.

Feeling accomplished, Alex and Sam were excited that we could proceed. There was still hope for their dream house! And then, Sam spoke a phrase I hadn't heard until that point: "My daughter will love this house! It's so much closer to her mom's so I'll get to see her a lot more". I froze. Sam had never been married or owned any other property (we asked during our screening process). We had failed to discover that he had a child. Did Sam have any support payment obligations? At the risk of exposing skeletons in the closet, I had to ask everyone on the phone line if I had consent to discuss their individual financial situation with everyone on the line. This file kept moving one step forward and three steps back and it was now impacting all our credibility. I advised them that I needed full and honest disclosure and started with Alex. "How much money do you get for your kids?" I asked. "I need everything from social assistance, to tax credits, to child support". She paused and then listed off another 2 sources of revenue that she was withholding from all of us. Phew! At least I had some additional income if it was required.

I then turned my attention to Sam. I asked him if he had any child or spousal support payments that he was responsible for. Again, the line went quiet for a bit longer than I expected. He exhaled and said "Yeah. I pay child support of $326/month". Silence ensued as I'm pretty sure neither of them knew each other's obligations or incomes. At this point, the realtor chimed in with her disappointment at all the time wasted and lack of full disclosure on both of their parts. "How is the mortgage broker supposed to secure you a mortgage when you lie, withhold information and keep changing the details that you've originally agreed on?"

Fast forward two months later and the situation had gotten worse. The house had reduced in price by a total of $100,000 and there was still no offer on the table. Alex had been laid off work but miraculously found another job closer to her new home. And *although we had satisfied almost all our conditions for the purchase mortgage, we were missing a key one: the downpayment confirmation which was supposed to come from the sale of the house.*

Since we can't control the market and this family had to close their purchase or risk losing their deposit, I had to think of the situation from a different perspective: the mom's. What if she bought out Alex and took the house over on her own?

I refinanced the current home which removed Alex from title and paid out her portion of her equity. Alex ended up with her downpayment AND removed from the obligations (title and mortgage), of her old house. Mom took the house off the market and kept it as a rental. It could carry itself while she rented an apartment closer to work. The purchase transaction for Alex, Sam and the kids closed (with a week extension), and a crisis was averted. We started off with a severe case of non-disclosure that was heading towards a nightmare situation. Add to that circumstances beyond our control (such as a market downturn), and you see how issues can escalate exponentially. By being able to leverage another character in this storyline, the deal was saved and a win-win situation was created for all.

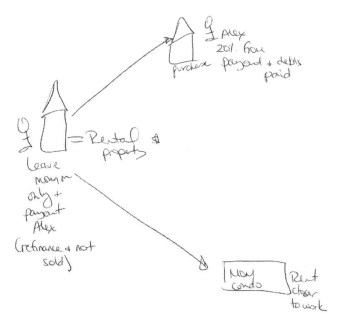

Figure H - Alex & Sam final solution

Chapter 3

Capacity: How You're Going to Make Your Payments

Income is a touchy subject. Some people are very forthcoming with it, almost to the point of being boastful. Whereas most, keep their information private and only delve the bare minimum to anyone who's inquiring. Some wear their job titles as a badge of honour. Others, for some reason, talk about their employment, or lack thereof, with a sense of regret. Regardless of how you feel about your salary or self-employed status, the fact remains that if you're going to apply for a mortgage, you'll have to discuss your income. In detail.

Income, or capacity (referencing our 5 C's of credit), is the factor of your borrowing profile which demonstrates to potential lenders your ability to make the payments. The rationale is that if you bring in $10 every month, we can't put you in a mortgage which has a payment of $7/month. We need to leave you with you some money to eat, get to work, and be able to buy a pair of shoes when you need to.

Once upon a time, we used to say that 3x your gross/before tax income was the approximate mortgage amount you could qualify for. If you made an annual salary of $50,000 you could assume that you could carry $150,000 mortgage. Add to that your downpayment and voila! You had your purchase price. Fast forward through the last decade where qualifying rules got easier, then harder and now to the infamous 'stress-test' that's in place. I can't even imagine a cheat-sheet formula. Once you factor in personal debt (which varies from one person to the next), condo fees (which have a huge variance for properties at the exact same price point), and an applicant's personal preference (house poor or 2 vacations a year), you have a lending environment where each application MUST be reviewed on its own merits.

Income is any form of money that you bring home through various sources. If you work for an employer, this could take the form of a salary, an hourly wage, a contract, or commissions. If you work for yourself, there are countless of ways you can be get paid for your work. Once we discuss it, I'll have a better idea of the papers I'll want from you. And be prepared because you will get asked for documentation. Sometimes it'll appear to be excessive so to get you ready, I've outlined a chart with the basic documentation requirements for the main sources of income. Remember, this isn't inclusive of all the items that can be requested of you. It's more of a starting point. The lender will always reserve the right to ask for more paperwork if they need further clarification of your income:

Table 1: Income sources and documents required

Employment Type	Documents Needed	
Salary (permanent employee)	Employment Letter	Recent paystub
I can	If you have incentives and/or bonuses which get paid annually, grab your last 2 years t4 slips so I can use that income in addition to your base pay.	If new on the job, your employment offer will also help.
Hourly Wage (permanent employee)	Employment letter. If you don't have a 2 year history with this employer, letter must state minimum number of guaranteed hours and your hourly rate.	Recent paystub
	Last two years t4 slips to factor in any overtime if it's something you consistently have	

Casual/ Seasonal employee	Employment letter	Recent paystub
	Last 2 years t4 slips or tax returns (T1 generals), with Notice of Assessments	
Self-employed or on contract withpayments made by an employer to your own corporation	Proof of business ownership i.e. business license, articles of incorporation	Last 2 years personal T1 generals and notice of assessments
	If incorporated, last 2 years company financial statements	Last 6 months business bank Account statements
Parental leave with previousposition guaranteed upon return	Employment letter confirming position, income and date of expected return	Last paystub prior to going onleave.
Support payments – child or spousal	Separation agreement and/orcourt order	Last 3 months bank statements to confirm deposits
Child tax credit	Summary tax statement confirming your kids' dates ofbirth and monthly payment	Last 3 months bank statements to confirm deposits

Pension income	Last year's t4 slips for all pension sources	Last 3 months bank statements to confirm deposits
Disability Income (permanent/long term)	Letter from insurer confirming length of time for income	Last 3 months bank statements to confirm deposits
Investment income/Capital gains	Current statement of accounts to confirm portfolio holdings	Last 2 years tax returns and notice of assessments to confirm if this income stream is a viable long term revenue source
International income (non-resident applicants)	Letter from employer or accountant/bank if self employed	Last 6-12 months bank statements to confirm deposits
Rental income	Lease	Income tax returns with rental schedule(s) if applicable
Tips/Gratuities/cash payment	Unless shown on a paystub and taxed at source, unfortunately, we won't be able to use this form of income.	

I need to understand the structure of your income so that I know what documentation will be conditioned by the lender and ensure we'll have it available. Let's pretend you tell me you make $65,000 a year and don't give me your documents. I may assume (one should never assume in this industry), it's a salary. I'm in for a very big surprise when you finally hand me your employment letter that confirms your base salary is $40,000 AND you're eligible for a performance bonus every year. You didn't lie to me when you said you earned $65k. You added in your bonus for that year and in fact, you really did make that money.

In my submission to the lender though, I have a 'salary' code for your income, which will cause the bank to condition for a job letter and paystub to confirm this data. We obviously can't satisfy this specific condition but we can still try to confirm your overall income by demonstrating a consistency for the last couple of years. If you send me your last two years' t4 slips or tax returns to show the lender that this is what you usually make every year we can now get around this hiccup. But here comes another problem: You've only been at this job for 14 months. Before this job, you were a 4th year university student with a part time job making a quarter of the money and oh….wait. You waived your financing condition on your purchase so you can no longer get out of this agreement. Add to this the fact that your closing date is in two weeks. I bet you're starting to get a stomach ache. This scenario is always good for a bout of nausea on both our parts and it's so preventable!

Had I collected your job letter and paystub during your pre approval phase or during your financing clause, I would have very quickly realized that you didn't have the documentation required to substantiate your income. Other alternatives could have been provided while still leaving you with the option to get out of your agreement. Or, I would have recommended you look for a place at a lower price point which your paperwork could support. There would be no need for us to be scrambling last minute to change lenders (to a higher rate option because you're now considered a higher risk), or adding on a co-signor for more income.

Sophie was a young professional in her early 30's and in the tech industry. She's viewed as a skilled employee by the banks. She was also a first time buyer. Her online application came through as salary employed and she sent in her job letter before leaving for a 2 week summer vacation to South America. Mortgage approval was finalized and her closing date was 3 months away so she felt she had plenty of time to deal with the remaining paperwork and conditions. When she finally sent in the rest of the documents for verification, I noticed that her paystubs confirmed an hourly wage and an inconsistent number of hours from pay period to pay period. Although her employment letter confirmed an *income* of $72,000, the paystubs had $38/hour for anywhere from 42 to 77 hours in a bi-weekly pay period. What Sophie didn't clarify was that she worked extra on the weekends for this same employer and was paid cash for that extra time. Her income on her application included **ALL** the hours she worked and the employer's letter confirmed her total pay. They weren't incorrect or maliciously trying to hide a pertinent fact. What they didn't know was that cash income not reported on paystubs and/or tax returns is not usable as income by lenders. Had I known this fact, I wouldn't have pre-approved Sophie for the amount I did. Usually, an error like this tends to happen when I don't receive paperwork up front but in her case, we had her job letter from the onset of the application with no paystubs until closer to closing. Only when the paystubs were handed in did I notice the difference and had to come up with an alternative solution.

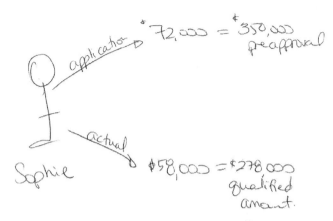

Figure I - Sophie's application situation vs. Sophie's real situation

Sophie needed a two day extension to close to her deal because her mortgage amount was reduced to the correct figure she could qualify for. This meant she now needed more downpayment to make up the difference and thankfully, her parents were able to help.

Louis was a young tradesperson in his early 20s, just starting in his tile setting career. He met with me to discuss his pre-approval plan and brought with him his job letter and paystubs. Right away I knew we were dealing with an hourly wage employee and this prompted me to ask him for his last 2 years t4 slips or notice of assessments. Because he probably put in a lot of overtime, the additional income could help him qualify for a bit more purchase price. I was able to confirm consistency in his income over the last 2 years and gave him his maximum recommended purchase price. After a few weeks of searching, he found his condo, got approved for his mortgage, signed all the paperwork and gave us the rest of the missing conditions on time. As far as I was concerned, the file was complete from my end. All I had to do was wait for his transaction to close in two months.

During that time though, Louis was hired on by another company and left the employer we had on file for him. He had thought about calling to advise us of this change but he assumed that because he gave us all the paperwork in November, that now in January, all was fine and he didn't have to update us with the new details. Louis was told (and forgot), that lenders will do a verbal verification of the employment letters closer to the closing date. This is done to ensure that you're still working at your job. When the lender called his employer and got confirmation that he was no longer working there, they were preparing to cancel his mortgage based on employment mis-representation. Understanding my clients' stories came in handy here. Rather than get caught off guard by a last minute approval cancellation (they thought he was unemployed 3 days prior to closing), I told them his story. I explained to the lender that as a skilled tradesperson, this borrower profile doesn't remain unemployed for long and that the client had probably changed jobs recently. Louis confirmed that he had indeed changed employers over the holidays and was making more money with more hours. The lender accepted a job letter from his new employer with a recent paystub. This time the phone call to the employer was confirmed. They used his previous lower amount of income (since there was no consistency at his higher wage), and he still qualified for his mortgage. His deal closed and another crisis was averted.

And finally, we have Jen and Wes, a couple in their mid-40s looking to refinance and pay out debt. During our meeting, my drawing looked like this:

Figure J - Jen & Wes

Wes disclosed his pay was salary as a full time permanent employee and although he made some income in bonuses, I didn't feel we needed to use it so I didn't ask for the additional paperwork. Jen on the other hand said she made $85k at a production company which she just started 3 months prior. Before taking on this role, she was working as a salary employee in the same field making $78k. Upon further probing, Jen mentioned that she's now on contract (1 year which could be renewed). This is the way her new employer pays employees. Her pay goes into her corporation which she set up for the sole purpose of this role. As a result, for lending purposes, she's considered a self-employed client because there's no guarantee of a contract renewal and she doesn't get deductions taken at source from her pay. I also didn't have a 2 year history for Jen at this income type or level. However, I was able to use her 2 year average in her last position because she was in the same industry and the income was lower. The mortgage was approved with a slight reduction to the principle amount originally requested and they proceeded to close because they still had enough money to do their debt consolidation.

The moral of the income/capacity story: no matter the type, amount or how long you're been making this income, disclose, disclose, disclose! It doesn't matter how minute or irrelevant you think the detail is because the more I know, the better I'm able to help you. It makes it less likely that something will complicate your closing date. And if I happen to ask you for a bit more paper (although it's the most annoying thing to dig up documents from 2 years ago), please help me out. Sometimes it's this one missing piece of paper that keeps you in A lending with best rates.

Unicorn Story - When it rains, it really does pour.

Especially for this guy. A few years ago, Sammy had it all. The wife and kids, a budding construction business and a coveted triplex in a downtown neighbourhood. The rent from the units was more than enough to cover the expenses and Sammy's family lived in their unit for almost nothing.

But when he didn't land the large contract that he thought was a done deal, all the plans that had been made with those funds, were gone. Unfortunately, they had started living as if the funds were guaranteed so the family was now in trouble. When I gave Sammy his first mortgage, the business was flourishing and there was ample work for both he and his wife, who worked as a designer on their job sites. Now, times were a bit tougher and they started missing some credit card payments because their priority was not to miss the mortgage payment. You see when there isn't enough money at the end of the month, you let the other things go. The line of credit, the credit cards, maybe a car payment and a utility bill. But you never miss the mortgage. By the time Sammy called me for help, he was behind on mortgage payments.

It was 4 years since he bought the house and now, Sammy's situation looked very different. He had closed the business and started working cash jobs on the side. He rented out their unit in their triplex and had moved his family into his mother's house. His wife found work at a local coffee shop. Income taxes hadn't been paid in a couple of years and CRA was threatening to put a lien on the home. Property taxes were behind 2 years and in 24 months with his current lender, he had missed 14 payments. 14 payments where he didn't have the money in his account and had to make arrangements for a later date. As a result of this repayment pattern, the lender wasn't offering him a renewal. They wanted a full payout.

When he finally reached out it was too late to try and keep him with a decently priced institutional alternate lender. His current lender wasn't giving him a renewal option so I had to move his mortgage somewhere else. Because no alternate lender would accept such a poor mortgage repayment history, I had no choice but to use a private lender. The only thing Sammy had going for him was his equity position. His property was worth $1.7million and when you added up all his outstanding debts, bills, taxes and the float fund he wanted, he only needed to borrow about $900,000. I arranged for a new private mortgage, to pay out EVERYTHING he owed. This included having the mortgage payments for the year deducted from the equity of his home. He would have no monthly payments for a year which would give him the opportunity to get back on his feet. This was a win-

win situation. Although the rate and fees on this mortgage were high because of his overall risk, the lender was protected by having their interest pre-paid up front. Sammy benefitted by having all his debt cleared up which would hopefully improve his credit score in the long run. He would have no mortgage payments for a year and that meant he could finally start saving some money. Sammy and his family used the equity in their home to buy them a year to breathe, re-organize, and emerge stronger. The plan was to get them back to a better priced lender next year.

Figure K - Sammy solution

Chapter 4

Capital: Your Skin in The Game

When deciding on purchasing a property, one of the numbers you have to look at is the downpayment, or the Capital in our 5 C's of credit. How much money do you have available to put towards this new purchase? Some people put the least amount of downpayment because they're first time buyers and haven't had the opportunity to save up. They take advantage of lending programs that can accommodate this. Others choose a lower downpayment although they have ample funds. They have other plans for their money and don't want it all tied up in this one property. And finally, there's a segment of buyers that put down ALL of their money. They want the least amount of mortgage possible which results in a lower monthly payment and interest cost savings in the long run.

Regardless of which type of buyer you are, the process is still the same when you buy a property: there's a deposit given with the offer and the difference of the downpayment will go to your lawyer a few days prior to your closing date. A common question I get asked is "does the deposit money count towards my downpayment?", and the answer is yes. If your total amount of downpayment is $50,000 and you put a $10,000 deposit with your offer, you only have $40,000 more to give your lawyer at closing. In addition, you'll also need money for the closing costs, which your lawyer calculates and advises you of.

Downpayment, much like income, also has its documentation requirements and clients sometimes find this a bit bizarre. In our initial conversation, I'll ask you about your intended downpayment and then I'll ask you for your bank statements. "But how would I be buying this property if I didn't have the money?", is the reaction I get sometimes, and it has nothing to do with doubting you. Canada has strict anti-money laundering laws which all lenders adhere to so at the foundation of the downpayment verification lies this basic fact: You can't use proceeds of illegal activities to purchase this property.

Some individuals use available credit as their downpayment source (credit cards or lines of credit). While this in itself isn't frowned upon, the non-disclosure of it is. As a mortgage broker, if you're using borrowed funds to purchase a property, I need to know if you can carry all the monthly repayments. There are programs in place to facilitate this type of transaction and all that's required is proof that you can carry the mortgage payments in addition to the added debt load of borrowing the downpayment.

What makes up a downpayment source and what are the minimum requirements?

Table 2 - Downpayment sources and examples of documents that could be requested

Downpayment Source	Documents Needed
1. Savings	3 months bank statements
2. Gift	Gift letter + funds in your account
3. Borrowed funds	Account statement confirming you have enough limit and minimum payment requirements
4. Sale of property	Firm sale agreement, mortgage statement and lawyer trust ledger to confirm net funds to you
5. Non registered investments	3 months account statements and proof of funds deposited into your chequing account
6. Registered investments	Same as above

7. Work bonus	pay stub showing the bonus being paid
8. Overseas funds	3 months bank account history in the originating country as well as all wire documents to show the funds being deposited into your Canadian bank account
9. Inheritance	copy of probated will and funds being deposited into your account
10. Lottery Winnings	Document from governing body i.e. OLG and deposit of funds into your account

Table 3: Minimum downpayment requirements

For properties < $500,000: minimum downpayment is 5% of the purchase price + closing costs

From $500,001 to $999,999: minimum downpayment is 5% of the first $500,000 and then 10% of the difference plus closingcosts

> $1million: minimum 20% downpayment + closing costs, however, some lenders require more based on their sliding scales for high-value properties

Owner occupied triplex or fourplex< $999,999: minimum 10% downpayment + closing costs

Owner occupied duplex < $999,999: minimum 5% of first $500,000 and 10% of the difference

Commercial property: Varies as this depends on the lender and type of property

Sounds simple enough, right? Yet sometimes….it gets messy.

Steve had it all planned out. The 20% downpayment on his new super cool downtown loft was coming from his stock portfolio. He had more than enough saved so he wasn't worried, even if the market dipped a bit. Mortgage was approved effortlessly and documents were signed with the only outstanding item being his downpayment confirmation. Not wanting to cash in his stocks yet because he would suffer some losses, Steve waited and waited. His closing date got closer and closer. We were all ready to go minus one condition: the liquidation of his investment into his account to show the lenders that the funds were available.

5 days before closing, Steve finally sent me his bank account statement showing the deposit of funds. What I saw made me freeze: Wire payment. Investments don't show up as wire transfers and are usually described as 'investment deposit' on a bank statement. A wire transfer tends to imply

money received from overseas which would now add another layer of paperwork to a file that was set to close with ease.

I called Steve and he confirmed that his investment advisor told him not to cash out if he didn't have to because of his losses on the downturned market. He reached out to his parents in Hong Kong and after explaining his situation to them, they happily gifted him the money he needed to close his first home. Breathing a sigh of relief, Steve now had the funds in his possession to finalize this purchase and sent me the confirmation. He didn't know that an international money transfer/wire had its own set of paperwork requirements. We didn't know there were funds being transferred from overseas.

I asked Steve to get his parents to sign a gift letter which was lender specific. In addition to the gift letter, Steve's lender also required a 3 month history of the gifted funds from the giftor because the amount was over $50,000. Steve wasn't amused. He didn't want to go back and ask his parents for their bank account history! We also needed paperwork showing the wire transfer so the lender could follow the funds from their origin to their final destination in Steve's account. What Steve and his parents thought was a simple solution to a glaring problem, turned out to be a bit of a paper nightmare. And it didn't have to be. Steve was getting frustrated because his lawyer was looking for instructions and was threatening extension fees if we didn't close on time. His parents in Hong Kong were upset that they had to provide their personal banking information which they felt was unnecessary. We were trying to manage a situation that could have totally been prevented if we were advised sooner of the plan to transfer money from overseas.

The file ended up closing on time and Steve didn't get charged any delay fees because my team and I orchestrated a communication plan with all parties:

1. While waiting for our documents from Steve and his parents, we connected with the lawyer and offered them a copy of the commitment letter. This would allow them to preview the conditions coming their way and the type of mortgage we put together.

2. We spoke to mom and dad directly explaining the situation from our perspective and the need to adhere to anti money laundering policies that are applicable to every lender. By offering them a direct line of communication to us, mom and dad by-passed sending their information through their son. This made them a bit more comfortable and gave us the bare minimum we needed.

3. We educated Steve, albeit a bit late, on the need for full transparency and disclosure. His #mortgagedont of not advising us of his plan was the potential demise of the mortgage we had approved for him with an 'A' lender.

It's not that Steve and his parents did anything wrong or that moving money from overseas isn't allowed. It's just a lengthier process to verify than locally sourced downpayment. It requires its own set of paperwork and we could have prepped Steve and his parents ahead of time so the process wouldn't have been so stressful for everyone involved.

Once again, the solution to avoid unnecessary hassles, stress and costs, is full disclosure. As we've seen numerous times, situations change. In a case like Steve's above, it wasn't a lack of disclosure at the beginning that caused him grief. It was an assumption that a problem was solved without giving us a heads up.

Unicorn Story - Always ask for more time than what you think you need.

Salima and Hussein had moved here from Europe and had been in Canada for just under 3 years. And it was a busy 3 years! They secured employment, set up their apartment, and had their first baby.

3 years later and baby number two on the way, they decided it was time to move out of their 1-bedroom apartment rental and get into a small house. They came to me for a pre-approval and brought their income documents up front for me to review. With both of them working salary, their incomes were easy to confirm. Our small challenge was with the downpayment because they hadn't quite saved it all yet. They were waiting for their year-end bonuses to come through along with a tax refund so I based the pre-approval on the assumption that they would have an $18,000 downpayment plus money for closing costs. I gave them the green light to put a conditional offer on a townhouse they fell in love with.

With the accepted offer and listing in hand, it didn't take long for the mortgage insurer to issue an approval. The only condition we had outstanding was the downpayment verification which we had no choice but to satisfy 3 days prior to closing. That's when the bonus at work was getting deposited. The clients came in excited to sign and go over the final details on next steps. They were given instructions on how to send me their last 3 months bank account statements for their savings the moment their bonus got deposited. And then, 3 days before the closing date, just as planned, the bank accounts came in. All 9 of them.

You can imagine my surprise when I realized that my team and I had to piece together 9 different bank accounts. They belonged to either Salima or Hussein, or jointly, or joint with her mom, or their young son. Most were savings accounts and two were chequing but what created the biggest issue was the movement of money.

When there's a large deposit into one account, we have to provide a 90 day history of the source of those funds. Our file closed January 30th and it was now January 27th. The lump sum of the bonus payment was easily confirmed via the paystub which it was paid on so we don't need a 3-month history of it. We knew the source was the employer. All of the bank accounts given to us as were as of November 1$^{st.}$ We had all of November, all of December and all of January as our 90-day history. However, when we looked at some of the November statements, there were large transfers in. The TFSA account had a transfer from the chequing account. The savings account had a transfer from another chequing account. This meant that we now needed a 90 day history of those transferred funds!

In one of those accounts we also noticed social assistance payments. Not only did we have to decipher the movement of funds, but we had to clarify whom the social assistance income belonged to.

We had 3 days until closing, a lawyer looking for documents and a nervous client worried about losing their deposit money. It took us a day (and a large board room table), to map out all the money movement from each account and clarify that the social assistance income was her mother's. The lender took a day to review the documents and sign off. After all was said and done, we had gone through a 6 month history of five of the accounts and 3 months history of the others. The family got their keys and moved in, just in time for the arrival of baby #2.

The #mortgagedont here was the rush to close the property and the assumption that just because you hand in paperwork, it gets looked at and processed immediately. My advice is to work with a determining date – be it a return from maternity leave, or in this case, waiting for a deposit of funds, to set your home's closing. We knew the date of deposit so the closing date should have been negotiated a bit longer after that to ensure everyone involved had the time required to do their part.

Chapter 5

A Credit History Is Plain and Simple, A Story

Everyone who has ever borrowed – a loan to purchase a car, a line of credit, or simply have a credit card, has a credit bureau. It contains all kinds of information such as your personal data, a timeline of addresses and employment, as well as credit accounts you currently own. It also may include historical accounts you've paid out and closed. A critical part of the credit bureau though, is the beacon score. A beacon score falls into 3 categories:

Great – a score over 700

Average – anything between 600 – 700

Low – less than 600.

Below, are examples of a fantastic credit bureau and a not so hot credit bureau.

CREDIT BUREAU VIEW
Gxxxxxx Mxxxx

USER REF. KxxxxxD   THIS FORM IS PRODUCED BY EQUIFAX C.I.S.   P.   1
MULTIPLE FILES INDICATOR: 0
EQUIFAX AND AFFILIATE BUREAUS – REFER CONSUMER INQUIRIES TO 1 – 800 – 465 - 7166

FN 00-00X8XX5-XX-0X1   UN 27XX6XX9X8   09/24/18   PG01

****
SAFESCAN WARNING:
  1 - NO FRAUD INDICATION WAS DETECTED
****

          BEACON SCORE: 732
          SERIOUS DELINQUENCY .
          TIME SINCE DELINQUENCY IS TOO RECENT OR UNKNOWN
          LEVEL OF DELINQUENCY ON ACCOUNTS.
          BANK. NAV. INDEX 2   SCORE: 972
          TOTAL BALANCE FOR OPEN BANK INSTALLMENT TRADES.
          UTILIZATION FOR BANK INSTALLMENT TRADES.
          TOTAL MONTHLY PAYMENTS.
          THICK PRIME CREDIT FILE SCORECARD.
          CRP   3.0   SCORE   782
          AVERAGE DECREASE IN RATING IN LAST 24 MONTHS.
          NUMBER OF TRADES 1 PAYMENT PAST DUE IN PREVIOUS 12 MONTHS.
          NUMBER OF TRADES OLDER THAN 12 MONTHS 30+ DAYS
          THICK PRIME CREDIT FILE
          ERS   2.0   SCORE   731
          NUMBER OF RATE 1 TRADES ON FILE.
          NUMBER OF TRADES ON FILE.
          WORST RATE EVER ON NATIONAL CARD TRADES.
          PRIOR DELINQUENCY THICK.

*MXXXXX, GXXXXXX SINCE 08/30/04 FAD 06/10/17
3X, AV LEXXXT, ETOBICOKE, ON MX1X1X STS RPTD 08/04
BDS – 12/25/19XX   SSS-5XX-XXX-1XX
*INQS
09/10/15   6XXBB2XX8   SIMPLII FI   CIBC   (888) 8XX-X7XX
      # INQS – 42
      ES – CITY OF TORONTO
SUMMARY 10/07 – 06/18, 1 – PR/OI, FB – NO, TOTAL – 6, HC$2K-$30K, 6-ONES.
*PUBLIC RECORDS OR OTHER INFORMATION
          10/13   SECLN MINISTRY GOVT SERV,   , 690XXX9XX BANK OF NOVA SCOTIA – ONTARIO CA
          U $20424
          SECURITY DEPOSIT UNKNOWN

*BUS / ID CODE	RPTD	OPND	H/C	TERMS	BAL	P/D	RT	30/60/90 MR	DLA
SCOTIALINE	(800) 3X8-X55X								
I*65XXBX06XX	06/18	03/08	24K		0	R1	01	00/00/00 72	06/18

ACCOUNT NUMBER XXX8X9X99143
          PRE HI RATES: R2 01/15
PERSONAL LINE OF CREDIT
MONTHLY PAYMENTS

CREDIT BUREAU VIEW

Gxxxxxx Mxxxxx

Default
52X Wxxxn Ave
Toronto, ON Mxx 1xx

SCOTIABANK VISA   (800) 3X8-X55X
I*65XXX28XX   06/18   10/11   2500   10   752   0   R1   00/00/00 72   06/18
ACCOUNT NUMBER XX8XX60X7X6
MONTHLY PAYMENTS
AMOUNT IN H/C COLUMN IS CREDIT LIMIT

CAPITAL ONE HBC   (866) 65X-7XXX
I*6XXOXX33   06/18   09/11   3800   0   R11   04/01/00 72   03/18
ACCOUNT NUMBER 2XXX78XXX980
        PREV HI RATES: R2 03/18, R2 06/16, R3 03/13.
MONTHLY PAYMENTS
AMOUNT IN H/C COLUMN IS CREDIT LIMIT

SCOTIA BANK   (888) 7XX-6XX9
I*65XXXX3XX8   05/18   10/13   30K   375   10K   0   I1   00/00/00 55   05/18
ACCOUNT NUMBER XXX23XXXX90
SECURED
MONTHLY PAYMENTS

AMERICAN EXPRESS   (800) 6XX-XX0X
I*65XXXX4XX11X 06/17   04/08   2700   0   0   R1   00/00/00 60   03/16
ACCOUNT NUMBER 3XXX7XX8XXX0
CLOSED AT CONSUMER REQUEST
ACCOUNT PAID

&
END OF REPORT
@&

CREDIT BUREAU VIEW
Mxxxxxx Nxxxx

MAY-24-2018   3:35:43 PM EST

Sherwood Mortgage Group
52X Wxxxn Ave
Toronto, ON Mxx 1xx

USER REF. Sxxxxxx   THIS FORM IS PRODUCED BY EQUIFAX C.I.S.   P.   1
MULTIPLE FILES INDICATOR: 0
EQUIFAX AND AFFILIATE BUREAUS — REFER CONSUMER INQUIRIES TO 1 – 800 – 465 - 7166

FN 00-00X8XX5-XX-0X1   UN 27XX6XX9X8   09/24/18   PG01

****
SAFESCAN WARNING:
  1 - NO FRAUD INDICATION WAS DETECTED
****

BEACON SCORE: 477
SERIOUS DELINQUENCY AND PUBLIC RECORD OR COLLECTION FILED.
BALANCE TO LIMIT ON BANK/NATIONAL, LOC OR OTHER REVOLVING ACCT TOO HIGH
AMOUNT OWED ON DELINQUENT ACCOUNTS.
NUMBER OF ACCOUNTS WITH DELINQUENCY.
BANK. NAV. INDEX 2   SCORE: 553
NUMBER OF TRADES 30+ DAYS IN LAST 12 MONTHS.
AMOUNT CURRENTLY PAST DUE.
NUMBER OF BANK REVOLVING TRADES BAD DEBT IN LAST 6 MONTHS.
THICK SUBPRIME CREDIT FILE SCORECARD.
CRP   3.0   SCORE 577
AGE OF MOST RECENT DEROGATORY PUBLIC RECORD.
AMOUNT CURRENTLY PAST DUE.
RATIO OF SATISFACTORY TRADES TO TOTAL TRADES IN LAST 24 MONTHS.
THICK SUBPRIME CREDIT FILE
ERS   2.0   SCORE 560
MONTHS SINCE MOST RECENT PUBLIC RECORD.
NUMBER OF PUBLIC RECORDS WITHIN THE LAST YEAR.
NUMBER OF TRADES 60+ DPD WITHIN THE LAST 2 YEARS.
DELINQUENT THICK.

*NXXXXX, MXXXXXX SINCE 12/11/91   FAD 06/18/18
X7, AV ALXXXN, TORONTO, ON MX1X1X TAPE RPTD 09/14
2XX, SXXXT RD, APT XX01,, TORONTO, ON MXX XXX TAPE RPTD 03/12
3XX4, GXXXXXT RD, MINDEN, ON XXX XXX TAPE RPTD 03/09
AKA – NXXXXXXX, MXXXXXXX,,XX
AKA – NXXXXXXX, MXXXXXXX,, M, XX
AKA – NXXXXXXX, MXXXXXXX,,XX
BDS – 11/14/19XX
*INQS - SUBJECT SHOWS   2 INQUIRIES SINCE 05/18
05/10/18   486XXBB2XX8   DLC MTG CXXX   (416) 2XX-X6XX
05/14/18   99XXXFXX5X3   SHERWOOD MORTGAGE   (416) 2XX-6XXX
10/17/17   48XXBXX7   TDCT TR 4XX5 VISA   (866) 4XX-X65X
03/22/17   4XXXBXX   CIBC   (416) 5XX-1XX1
07/20/16   4XXCXXX   TDCT TR 4XX5 VISA   (866) 4XX-X65X
      # INQS – 101
      ES – GALLERY ARTIST
      ES – BFS OWNER
      ES - ACTOR
SUMMARY 08/03 – 05/18, 1 – PR/OI, FB – NO, TOTAL – 15, HC$300-$185K, 1-ZERO, 11-ONES, 3-NINES.

Equifax Canada Inc
MC02-2X7X0

CREDIT BUREAU VIEW
Mxxxxxx Nxxxx

MAY-24-2018   3:35:43 PM EST
Sherwood Mortgage Group
52X Wxxxn Ave
Toronto, ON Mxx 1xx

*PUBLIC RECORDS OR OTHER INFORMATION
     05/18 UP CL*CASH FLOW RECOVERIES, $978, BRN -- UTRAMAR, DLA-11/17, BAL-5978, ACC-7XXX578

*BUS / ID CODE	RPTD	OPND	H/C	TERMS	BAL	P/D	RT	30/60/90 MR	DLA
CIBC	(416) 9XX-4XX0								
I*48XXXB15XX	05/18	08/03	10K		0	0	R1	00/00/00 62	03/17
ACCOUNT NUMBER XXX....420									
PERSONAL LINE OF CREDIT									
MONTHLY PAYMENTS									
S.CARTES DESJARDINS (800) 3XX-3XX0									
I*00XX0X2XX76	05/18	10/10	1000		0	0	R1	04/00/00 72	11/15
SCOTIALINE	(800) 3X8-X55X								
I*65XXBX06XX	05/18	11/04	4605	50	4604	540	R9	00/00/00	08/17
ACCOUNT NUMBER XXX...405									
PRE HI RATES:	R5 04/18, R5 03/18, R5 02/18								
ACCT ASSIGNED TO THIRD PARTY FOR COLLECTION									
ACCOUNT CLOSED									
SCOTIABANK VISA	(800) 3X8-X55X								
I*65XX28XX	05/18	03/09	2154	57	2153		R1	03/01/00 72	05/18
ACCOUNT NUMBER XXX...697									
ACCOUNT CLOSED									
MONTHLY PAYMENTS									
TD CREDIT CARDS	(800) 9XX-8XX2								
I*60XX44	03/18	03/14	17K		19K		R9	00/00/00	03/17
ACCOUNT NUMBER XXX...686									
PREV HI RATES:	R5 02/18, R5 01/18, R5, 12/17								
WRITTEN-OFF									
CLOSED BY CREDIT GRANTOR									
AMERICAN EXPRESS	(800) 6XX-XX0X								
I*65XXXX4XX11X	05/17	04/08	11K	65	150	0	R1	03/00/00 53	04/16
ACCOUNT NUMBER 3XXX7XX8XXX0									
PREV HI RATES:	R2 02/16, R2 06/15, R2 01/15								
CLOSED AT CONSUMER REQUEST									
MONTHLY PAYMENTS									
CAPITAL ONE HBC	(866) 65X-7XXX								
I*6XXOXX33	05/18	09/11	7500		0		R1	08/02/00 41	03/18
ACCOUNT NUMBER 2XXX62XXX580									
PREV HI RATES:	R3 10/15, R2 09/15, R3 02/15.								
CLOSED AT CONSUMER REQUEST									
ACCOUNT PAID									
I* BB	09/14		185K	958	0	0	M1	00/00/00	09/14
ACCOUNT PAID									
MORTGAGE									
&									
END OF REPORT									

Figure L1 & L2 - Example of a great credit bureau and a not so great bureau

There are numerous theories about how a beacon score is arrived at and although I don't have the magic formula, the following are common consumer thoughts on credit ratings:

1. True or False? Inquiries lower your credit score

Answer: Both.

Whenever someone pulls your credit bureau, it's reported as an inquiry. Many people believe that the more inquiries you have, the lower your score goes and this has some merit. Personally, I'm of the belief that a few credit pulls during expected life events i.e. applying for a student loan, financing a vehicle and buying a home, don't impact your overall credit score. If you think about it, there's usually a bit of time in between events and you may have a couple of credit checks per lender because you're shopping around. Someone with a great credit score won't get pushed into a worse scoring with credit inquiries. Usually for these types of clients, an inquiry or two doesn't impact their beacon score at all. For this type of borrower, believing numerous inquiries lowers your credit score, is false.

Where you do run into issues is when you have a borderline score to begin with AND there are problems with your financing. Examples include that you're not getting the rates you'd like (often as a result of your overall credit profile). Or the application fell apart at one lender and now you're viciously scrambling to put your deal together with another lender so you've got many applications out simultaneously. As a mortgage broker, if I see many inquiries from lenders and mortgage brokerages in the last 2 weeks, red flags go up. A borrower looking to just shop rates is confident in their credit score and get rates quoted without an actual credit check. Someone with numerous recent inquiries has run into a challenge and is now frantically looking for a solution. This type of borrower will also usually have an average beacon score. As a result of all the inquiries, they may get bumped into a lower scoring bracket. For this borrower, inquiries lowering your credit score is definitely true.

2. True or False? Having a lot of credit facilities is beneficial.

A credit bureau is a record of your repayment behaviour so with individuals who have numerous credit accounts, we tend to see the following two types of borrowers:

> a. Ample credit available = Many credit accounts but the client only uses a main credit card and maybe a line of credit. In this case, although the borrower has ample credit available to him, he's only operating two accounts. I, as the mortgage broker, will review his activity on these accounts because the others

will all be stale-dated with no current update on them. Having access to credit and not using it shows that you're responsible and not reliant on it. It won't necessarily increase your credit score. It definitely won't decrease it either.

b. Credit dependent = Many credit accounts with all of them used and most often, at full capacity. In this case, our applicant has too many accounts and running them at their limits which will definitely impact her overall credit score negatively. On initial review, the lenders and I will get the impression that she's living beyond her means. She's relying on her credit cards and lines of credit to support her. It may indicate that her income isn't enough to cover her expenses and her credit score will be reflect this behaviour.

Answer: False. There is no benefit to having numerous credit accounts unless you're revolving them responsibly.

3. True or False? Consumer proposals are not the same as bankruptcies.

There have been plenty of times where an applicant has told me "but I didn't do a full bankruptcy. It was only a proposal!". There seems to be a common misconception that consumer proposals are like a fender bender. They can be easily fixed with no impact to the operation of the vehicle. Bankruptcies on the other hand, are seen as a full on multi-car pile-up on the highway with your car being the worst hit.

The fact is that both of these types of credit challenges are seen in a negative light by lenders for the same reason: The borrower failed to make payments as initially agreed. Although we all acknowledge that in a proposal one is making arrangements to pay off some of their obligations (and most do so successfully), it's still only a partial payment. Hence why it's put in the same category as a bankruptcy, which is a complete write off of all obligations.

A lender is looking for their mortgage to get paid as agreed throughout the entirety of its lifespan. Although they'll lend to previous bankrupt/consumer proposal applicants, they'll have stricter requirements for these borrowers.

Answer: False. For mortgage lending purposes, consumer proposals and bankruptcies are treated the same.

4. True or False? I'm only a co-signor so that shouldn't be counted as my debt.

This is one of my personal favourites and it usually tends to hurt my first time buyers. Imagine being all excited that you've found your first place but you've completely forgotten that you co-signed for your sister's car loan. Her $580/month payment just cost you your approval because once I add it into your liabilities, you don't qualify for your own loan.

"But my sister makes this payment!", you say in despair, "it's her car!!".

And although I agree with you and believe you, unfortunately, in the eyes of the car loan issuer, you're both responsible. Should your sister wake up one day and decide not to make her payment, that lender is going to be looking for you to make it. Hence why we have to include it in our ratios. There are work-arounds for this situation, which we offer and you can discuss with your sister. In the meantime, it's included as your debt which makes our answer: False.

5. True or False: I paid that delinquent account! It shouldn't be on my bureau anymore.

Bankruptcy information tends to fall off your credit bureau 7 years after you're discharged. But what about those pesky collection accounts? Or that judgement from the dentist on an account that you didn't agree to pay because you weren't happy with the work? Did you open up a credit card without realizing there was an annual fee, which you later disputed and decided that you weren't going to pay it? All these smaller credit challenges, which are often one-time incidents, have a way of coming back to bite you when you least expect it.

So although you've paid these accounts to $0, the derogatory information will still be displayed in your credit history. A written off account with a 'paid' or $0 balance is looked at more favourably than that same account with a current outstanding balance on it.

Answer: False. Just because you pay off a delinquent account (collection or judgement), doesn't mean the account drops off your credit score immediately.

6. True or false: That's not my account. I don't have any_____

This one is a bit tricky and the following are situations which can cause this reaction:

> A. Family members with the same name: We see this happen often when John Smith applies for a mortgage and his dad, John Smith Sr., has credit accounts which make it onto his son's bureau. Usually the two are still living at the

same address. In this case, we try to add more of our applicant's information on the credit profile inquiry i.e. SIN number. If that fails, a phone call by you to the credit bureau issuer will usually suffice for them to pull the two profiles apart and have Jr.'s download on its own next time.

B. Account has been paid but not reported: Sometimes you've paid out a car loan but the financing company forgets to report the last payment to the credit bureau and show the account as paid/closed. This is an easy fix because all that's required is documentation from the finance company confirming you don't owe anything. We can then proceed with the application. A good practice is for you to send this documentation to the credit company and they can update the information on your file so it doesn't come up again in any future applications.

C. The account has been sold/new lender and you don't know this creditor: Did you ever take advantage of a 'do not pay until……' finance option with 0% interest? Many people have purchased furniture and electronics under these plans and only know the retailer (not the actual financing company). After some careful thought and digging up of original contracts, the mystery is solved by the borrowers and the account is no longer disputed.

So the answer to the question is: Both. Good news is that there are easy fixes for this concern and it shouldn't impact the mortgage application.

So what's the point to having a credit score? There are so many variables that impact it and each lender has different minimum requirements. First of all, it's never just about the score. There have been plenty of times when an applicant has a 700 beacon score but there are spotty late payments throughout their history. Maybe even a collection or two that have been paid. Looking at the score only, I may assume that this is a responsible borrower. However when I look at the details, I see someone who makes sloppy payments. Sometimes the slow repayment pattern is in the summer where I may assume again, they're on vacation, not paying attention to details such as due dates. There have also been situations where applicants have a 620 credit score and have immaculate repayment history with minimal debt obligations. The score is on the lower end of average because the credit bureau reflects a $200,000 secured line of credit that's used to its full limit. This should be recorded as closed because the sale of that property occurred last week but the credit bureau hadn't been updated yet. This is why it's important that I look at the whole picture and present it to lenders correctly. This picture paints out a timeline of how you, the borrower, has managed their debt load. What kind of debt have you carried? Have you paid on time? Are there numerous inquiries? Does the employment and address on the credit bureau match the application? What limits have you been granted on your current cards and lines of credit? Based on all this information, your mortgage lender will decide if they want to approve your application. Good credit shows that you pay as agreed and are responsible. Bad credit paints a different picture. If you can't manage a $2500 credit card, how are you going to manage a quarter of a million dollar loan?

How about those who haven't had the opportunity to establish any credit yet? Usually, these are students right out of school or new immigrants to the country. Students, by virtue of their age, aren't punished for their lack of credit because lenders understand they haven't had the opportunity to do obtain any yet. As a result, a younger applicant with no credit history will almost always be asked for a co-signor until they establish their own credit score and can qualify on their own. An immigrant on the other hand may not have the luxury of a local co-signer with credit so for these borrowers, we have different solutions. If they come from a country where they have credit bureaus i.e. USA, we'll use their international credit report in lieu of a Canadian report. The applicant would order their profile online and submit it with the rest of their documentation. If they come from a country where credit isn't a way of life, the New to Canada programs will allow for other sources of credit worthiness. This can include a bank reference letter from their home bank and a 6-12 month Canadian account history showing payments to monthly obligations such as rent, utilities or cell phones.

Since there are options for those with limited credit and the rest of us have our credit histories, how can a mortgage approval be impacted based on credit once it's granted?

Lainey, was 25 years old and purchased her first condo from a reputable builder in North York which wasn't scheduled to close for another 18 months. As a buyer for a large retailer, she had a salary of $50,000 and was able to qualify for her $180,000 mortgage easily, without any issues. The downpayment came from her savings and was already given to the builder in incremental deposits. All she had to do for the next year and a half was work, save and wait for her closing date to arrive. Her cute one bedroom unit was 640 square feet with a 50 square foot balcony on the 18th floor, overlooking a ravine. She would catch some phenomenal sunsets in the summer. She started imagining hosting dinners for her friends and having her nieces for sleep overs. Every time she went out to the mall, she would pick up a few little items for her new place. She figured that a little bit here and there over the next 18 months would be a manageable expense while still saving to purchase her big ticket item furnishings. Her closets at her mom's place (where she was currently living), were filling up with linens and kitchen items, all purchased during sale events. Lainey prided herself on being a frugal shopper.

Then came the first notice of delay. "Great", thought Lainey, "I have more time to pay this stuff off". A few months later a new job offer came up which would pay her $10,000 more per year on her base salary plus give her some incentives. She would have to move to her employer's head office in Mississauga which now meant she needed a car. Thinking that her extra income would offset the cost of the car, Lainey went out and purchased a vehicle with really low interest financing and a monthly payment of $320. Life was good. She had an exciting new job and was slowly outfitting her condo with the stuff she needed. Patiently, she waited for her closing date to arrive so she could move out and be on her own.

During boxing week that year, she happen to notice her favourite furniture store having a huge sale. Her closing date was targeted for that following summer. When would she ever have this chance to buy her larger items at such a low cost? Taking advantage of the sales and the 0% financing for the furniture, Lainey purchased ALL her big ticket items and felt great about it. She could now spend the next 7 months saving money to pay for all her furniture as it came due in 2 years when the interest special expired. She didn't have to worry about anything else other than working and saving. Her furniture was being delivered to her mom's storage unit and all her other smaller items were bought and on hand.

The final closing date was July 17th and Lainey reached out to me to finalize her mortgage details. Because her application had expired due to all the building delays, we had to start from the beginning. Income was better than we had before. However, when I pulled her credit bureau, I was shocked. What should have been an easy re-approval, ended being a complicated mess with co-signers because Lainey had accumulated $60,000 in debt in the last 2 years. Between her car, furnishings, and a couple of trips she went on, Lainey no longer qualified for her mortgage. Although her place was well furnished and she got in some travel, mom and dad had to co-sign for her mortgage.

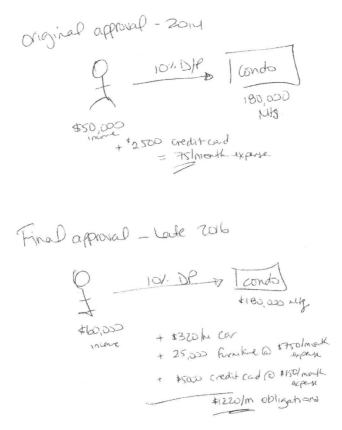

Figure M - Lainey's mortgage structures

Rob applied for a refinance with me but we couldn't close the deal until his basement renovation was completed by the insurance company. During a storm, his basement flooded. A city tree in his front yard had grown roots in his old clay pipes and caused a backup. The whole process was scheduled to take about 4-6 weeks between clean up, pipe replacement and basement finishing so we pushed the closing date out an additional 2 months. While he was busy working and dealing with the basement renos, Rob put aside his bills thinking that he would pay them closer to the due date. He was hoping that we could wrap up the refinance at that same time and save him the effort of making the payments. But the due date came and went, and he had forgotten that he hadn't made his minimum payment. Once he remembered, he ran to the bank and paid them in full. Although his balances were now zero, he hadn't made the minimum payment by the due date (as agreed). The creditor impacted his credit score by rating him an R2. Credit scores range from 1 (never late), to 9 (written off) and the R2 was reflective of his 30 days late. Once we coupled this with the fact that Rob's application was expiring because he wasn't ready to close, we had a problem. I re-did his application a couple of weeks later when the basement work was fully completed. His original credit score of 625 was reduced by 30 points at 595. No longer a viable borrower for his original lender, Rob's options were to either wait another few months and hope his score would increase, or pursue an alternate lending option with higher pricing. He chose the higher priced lender because he wanted to roll all his debt into one monthly payment.

Although the initial delay of the file closing due to the basement flooding was nothing anyone could control, his bill repayment behaviour was. Even though you have an approval secured, your credit score coupled with a longer closing, could impact your ability to close with your original lender. Always make sure to stay on top of your debt obligations.

Chapter 6

Do the Appraisal Up Front. It's Worth It.

Disclaimer:* *This chapter is a bit technical, so it'll read a bit different than the rest of the book as I take you through calculations and risk factors associated with property types.*

Location, location, location is the widely quoted golden rule of real estate. In addition to the location though, did you know that the **TYPE** of property you're interested in mortgaging will affect your application? Factors such as interest rates and maximum mortgage amounts are all impacted on certain features of the property. Whether you're buying a new home or looking to restructure your current mortgage, the details of your property will be analyzed.

Collateral, or the last C in our credit analysis, is the security that the mortgage is being loaned against. In simple terms, the lender is taking your property as collateral until you pay off your mortgage. If there are issues in repayment, the lender has a way to recoup their loan via power of sale or foreclosure methods. These are beyond the scope of this book and will not be discussed in detail. So although credit and income is what you're bringing to the table to prove your ability to repay, the property will also be assessed by the lender to ensure it meets their standards.

Property types are usually split into two main areas:

Table 4: Residential property type breakdown by intended occupancy

Owner Occupied	Rental
Condo Apt/Townhouse	Owner occupied with rental units
Single family house	All rental
2nd home	Mixed-use (commercial and residential)
Vacation property	
Multi-plex	

Let's consider a single family home as a basic application for a mortgage request. For these files, I have to demonstrate that you qualify to carry a mortgage on a property which is your primary residence. Qualifying means that you can afford the payments and looks at the following variables:

$$Q = \frac{\text{Monthly mortgage payment} + \text{Monthly heat} + \text{Monthly property tax}}{\text{Borrower gross monthly income}}$$

$$Q = \leq 39\%$$

Figure N - Qualifying calculation

This 39% represents the amount of your gross income that the lenders are comfortable with you spending on your shelter costs.

Once we change the property type though, we now have to look at extra pieces of information which impact the risk assessment:

Condo Townhouse or Condo Apartment

$$\text{Condo} + Q = \frac{\text{Same figures as figure P} + \text{monthly condo fees}}{\text{Same income as above}}$$

$$Q = \leq 39\%$$

Figure O - Condo calculations

Even though a condo or townhouse is still considered a single family home, there's a difference in the qualifying process because of the additional condo fees. This additional expense will impact the amount of mortgage you qualify for. In a pre-approval situation, a purchaser will get one recommended maximum purchase price for a freehold property and another for a condo apartment/townhouse.

Vacation home or second property

If you're looking for financing on a vacation property (usually a property used by the family on a seasonal basis), or a secondary home (a residence purchased for a member of the family i.e. student away at university or elderly parent), there's a slight difference in qualifying. Even though we're still dealing with single family properties, you're adding an additional place with its own expenses so the qualifying becomes a bit more complex.

$$Q = \frac{\text{Same monthly expenses as figure P} + \text{monthly mortgage} + \text{monthly heat} + \text{monthly property taxes} + \text{monthly condo fees of your current home}}{\text{Same monthly borrower income as figure P}}$$

$$Q = \ \leq 39\%.$$

Figure P - Vacation property calculations

Comparing these different types of owner occupied single family properties, you see that there are small calculation differences when it comes to qualifying. This impacts the amount of mortgage you'll be able to get approved for.

But what if there's potential for rental income from the property?

Then the process starts again with the question of "are you living in this rental property in one of the units or are you leasing it out 100%"

Multi-residential

To be considered under residential financing (as opposed to commercial lending), there should be no more than 4 units in these types of properties. These homes can be 2 unit houses – a main residence plus basement apartment or a house legally zoned as a duplex. They can also be triplexes or fourplexes. More than 4 units and the property may fall in commercial lending with different qualifying requirements and pricing.

To qualify for one of these properties the question now becomes if you're going to be residing in it. If you're not occupying any of these units as your principle residence it becomes a full rental property. I factor in your current shelter costs from where you live (your mortgage payment at home or your rent), and the maximum rents from this property (all the units will be generating income). The lenders vary in the amount of rental income they use to qualify your mortgage as they rarely use 100% of it. They like to show funds aside to cover expenses not used in the qualifying ratios i.e. property maintenance, utilities and vacancy.

Owner occupied

| Tennant |
| You |
| Tennant |

$$Q = \frac{\text{Same costs as figure P}}{\text{Same borrower monthly gross income + 50\% of rent from upper and lower units}}$$

$$Q = \leq 39\%.$$

Full rental

| Tennant |
| Tennant |
| Tennant |

$$Q = \frac{\text{Same costs as figure P + your monthly costs of your residence}}{\text{Same income as figure P + 50\% rent from all units}}$$

$$Q = \leq 39\%.$$

Figure Q - Multi residential calculations

Errors start happening when a borrower believes that their rental properties actually help them qualify for more mortgage. Let's assume you own a single unit rental with the following parameters:

- $1000/month in rent

- The mortgage payment is $600/month

- heating is $100/month

- property taxes are $150/month

- You have an annual salary of $60,000

Your own residence costs you:

- $1100/month mortgage payment

- $100/month heat

- $250/month property taxes

Table 5: Your actual monthly cash flow situation versus what the lender sees for the rental property:

Actual	Lender perspective
$1000 rent	**$500 rent**
-$600 mortgage	-$600 mortgage
-$100 heat	-$100 heat
-$150 property tax	-$150 property tax
= $150 monthly cash flow	= **-$350** monthly cash flow

You assume that your income will have $150/month added to it to help you qualify for your new purchase. Based on the lender's perspective, you're actually short $350/month to carry your rental property. This means that you now have $350 less each month to help you pay your own obligations.

If we look at the qualifying ratios, the 2 situations look as follows.

Your actual situation:

$$Q = \frac{\text{rental property } (600+100+150) + \text{your home } (1100+100+250)}{\text{Your income } (\$60,000/12) + \text{rental } \$1000}$$

$Q = (\$850 + \$1450) / \$6000 = 38.3\%$. **Deal qualifies!**

Lender qualifying ratio:

$$Q = \frac{\text{rental property } (600+100+150) + \text{your home } (1100+100+250)}{\text{Your income } (\$60,000/12) + 50\% \text{ of rental } \$500}$$

$Q = (\$850 + \$1450) / \$5500 = 41.8\%$ **Deal doesn't qualify!**

As you accumulate more and more real estate, the more complicated your story becomes. Clients with rentals assume when the rent covers the expenses, the property won't have a negative impact on their application. Understanding that the lender is taking only a portion of the rent against 100% of the expenses will help you realize that you may present a lower cash flow and be approved for a reduced amount of mortgage.

MIXED-USE PROPERTIES

The more complex the property becomes, the more thorough we have to be with our information to our lender. Let's take a look at a mixed use property which has a commercial component on the main floor and a residential unit or two on the upper level. You may be a business owner looking to purchase your premises and stop paying rent. This would be considered owner occupied. It may be a perfect scenario for you because the business can operate on the lower level, while you live and/or rent in the residential units upstairs. Alternatively, you may be looking to expand your real estate portfolio. You may want to delve into a commercial property so you'll be looking to rent out all units in the property for maximum cash flow. This would be considered a full rental.

In order to secure the best financing solution for you, I want to know:

1. Who's occupying the residential units? If they're being rented out, the owner's own shelter costs have to be factored in when we qualify the

application. If however the owner is living there, we don't have rental income from that specific unit but we also don't have to consider any additional monthly expenses from another residence.

2. Is the owner occupying the commercial space with her business (in which case there would be no additional rental income to help qualify), or is the space being rented to a third party (in which case we now have some rental income to help this borrower qualify)?

3. How much experience does the borrower have in operating this type of property?

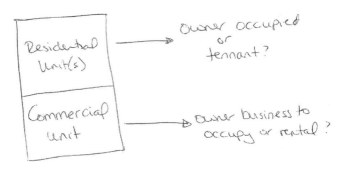

Figure R - Mixed use property questions

Outside of qualifying to purchase or refinance a property, other factors that influence the analysis of the collateral, are:

Location

- Are there any detrimental factors i.e. industrial areas nearby or environmental concerns/contamination from neighbouring businesses?

- What's the population of the area?

- Is the property well and septic or is it on municipal water and sewage?

- Are there any special assessments or lawsuits that impact the financial well-being of your specific building and condo corporation?

Use

- Is the property zoned as a legal single family home but you've added locks to each door and made it student housing?

- Are you on a main road in between mixed use properties occupying a two story mixed use building as your main residence?

- Do you have a small bungalow on a large lot in an urban setting? This appraisal may give all the value of the property to the land and a little to no portion on the actual house

Tools, such as appraisals and home inspections, give us some of the information we need to analyze the property but the need for accuracy is imperative when I present your application to a potential lender. Especially if you're an investor with a larger portfolio. You're the key to providing all the pertinent information we need to describe the property and its use. Lenders aren't in the business of taking over people's homes and nor are they interested in going through power of sale proceedings. When they review a mortgage application though, they have to look at the property from that potential loss angle. Will they be able to sell this property and recoup their funds in a timely manner if the borrower stops paying?

Although we all like to think we have the best home on the block, we have to be realistic in terms of what our house is valued in comparison to the recent sales of similar properties. An appraisal done at the start of the application process is highly recommended as it'll confirm the figures were dealing with. Not only does the appraisal confirm a value for us to use and calculate your mortgage amount on, it also describes the property and neighbourhood. It states any positive or negative influences which may impact its marketability and it's an important tool in property analysis. It can also be one of the most common items jeopardizing financing.

Joe and Helen were buying a second home after having sold their existing place. They wanted to upgrade because now they had a child and were really trying to get into certain neighbourhood with great schools and access to transit. But so were three other families. Multiple offer situations are common in these scenarios. It's a high stress time where buyers want to go in with the least amount of conditions in order to be competitive and secure their new home. Most of the time, if the listing realtor is expecting multiple offers, a home inspection will be provided on site but a home inspection is not an appraisal. An inspection tells you the nitty-gritty nuts and bolts of the operation of the house and whether or not you're going to need to replace anything soon i.e. plumbing. The appraisal on the other hand, as noted above, comes up with a value for the house (in comparison to other sales in the neighbourhood during a recent timeframe).

By the time they decided to put in an offer, Joe & Helen were bidding against four other families. They really really really really wanted this house. They wanted this house so badly that they were willing to overpay a little just so they could clinch it. They had been falling in love with homes and putting in offers only to end up losing to someone paying more and now the perfect house in the perfect location, was within grasp. They could visualize where the Christmas tree and decorations were going. They saw their entire extended family enjoying a meal at the large table in the dining room with the bay window and wainscotting. They weren't letting this one go! Glancing at the listing, they noticed that the asking price was $799,000 and they were thinking of going in aggressively at $815,000. They thought this would seal the deal because they were offering more than asking price but unbeknownst to them, all the other couples had done the same thing. Before they knew it the price was up to $840,000. "What's a few thousand dollars more for decades of life and memories in this property?", they thought. "It'll be fine in the long run". They signed off at $845,000 and got the house.

But was it fine for the mortgage? Joe and Helen didn't realize during this emotional battle that they would have some issues with their pre-approved mortgage. Without having a financing condition on the purchase there was no way to back out of the deal if they hit any snags. They were comfortable enough during the pre-approval phase based on their sale proceeds, income and credit that they felt their chances would be hindered if they put in the financing clause. Although warned about the impact of a lower appraisal, they still decided to proceed.

Cue the snag.....The Appraisal.

When the report came in, the supported value of this house was $805,000 and NOT the $845,000 they purchased for. Remember that the house was listed originally at $799,000 (in line with the appraised value), however Joe & Helen intentionally overpaid to win the bidding war. Their mortgage, which was approved for 80% of their offer of $845,000, now had to be reduced because lenders use the LOWER of the purchase price or appraised value. They were going to have to top up their downpayment amount in order to cover the difference. Would they have enough funds from the sale?

Originally, the approved mortgage amount was 80% of $845,000 = $676,000. This made their downpayment a total of $169,000 + closing costs.

Once we revised the figures to reflect 80% of the appraised value of $805,000, the mortgage amount was reduced to $644,000. This increased their downpayment to $201,000 + closing costs. That's a difference of $32,000.

Re-running the figures on their sale confirmed that Joe and Helen would net $225,000. This was just enough to cover the downpayment and closing costs. With the original approval, they would have had extra funds left over after the downpayment to top up their savings plans. Now, that wasn't possible. They were grateful they had enough funds from the sale but can you imagine if they were first time buyers with no access to additional funds and had waived their financing condition?

As we round up the 5 C's of credit with collateral, it's important to note that the lenders do pay attention to the property which they're registering their mortgage on. Applicants are stressed out over their incomes not being enough to qualify for their dream home, or their credit not meeting a minimum standard for best pricing. They often dismiss the importance that the real estate plays in the decisioning of their file.

Unicorn story – Diane

She was beyond pleasant and calm every time she spoke to me. Diane was introduced to us by a past client and she had some complicated financing requirements. A nurse by trade, Diane had spun off a side business for senior home care. She was doing quite well with 3 locations, 4 properties of her own and a large piece of land she was looking to develop up north.

Since having gone self-employed though, Diane was realizing that it was tougher to get a mortgage. As her 'A' mortgages were coming up for renewal, she wanted to refinance them and pull out money to inject into her thriving business. There was always some modification that had to made to a property or some more equipment to purchase. Her income tax filings were up to date and she didn't claim much personal income. Out of her 3 existing mortgages, only the one on her primary residence could be refinanced with an 'A' lender under a self-employed program.

With the transaction completed by her local bank branch and some funds in her account to continue growing her little empire, Diane set her sights on refinancing her rental properties. Both were large stately homes just outside of Toronto and were bringing in good rental income. She gave me a call, explained her situation and booked a meeting to bring me all her paperwork. It was evident that she would need an 'alternate' mortgage solution. The size of the loans she was requesting and the fact that she didn't declare a lot of personal income on her tax returns made her better suited for a non-bank mortgage.

When she walked in, we definitely noticed that she had a glowing presence. It was very obvious from her demeanour that she was a perfect fit for the caregiving industry. With her big smile and even bigger tote bag filled with organized paperwork, she and I sat down for the first of many, many meetings and phone calls together. We went through the motions: completed the application, got an approval on each property, dealt with the conditions and compliance paperwork and were ready to close once the appraisals came through. Everyone was happy that these somewhat complicated files were coming to a close.

Until the appraisals were completed.

Mortgage approval one was based on a property value of $1,200,000 for rental house A. She constantly reminded us that this was on the conservative end because the neighbours all sold for $1.35 million. They were smaller so $1.2mil for her property in a bit worse condition, was fair. With that value, I planned to get her existing mortgage paid out and give her approximately $200,000 in hand to complete the work she wanted to do to update the home. The appraisal though, came in at $950,000 which now only left her with net proceeds of about $23,000 once we paid out her existing mortgage, lending fees and legals. A chart breaking down the original plan vs the actual reality we were in, is below:

	Original proposal	Actual funding
Value of property	$1,200,000	$950,000
Mortgage amount (Maximum 75% of Appraised value)	$900,000	$712,500
Existing mortgage	$680,000	$680,000
Net funds after	$205,000	$22,800

How could she have been so far off? It turns out that she only focused on the higher end of the sales spectrum in her area, and not the properties that sold for less. Once we reviewed the comparable *sales in the appraisal report and engaged the appraiser she conceded that the value, although much lower than what she would have liked, was fair. The decision now remained for her to make. Was it worth it to lose her current 'A' priced mortgage at the bank (which she could still just renew with 'A' rates at her existing lender and take no money out)? Or, did she risk going to an alternate lender which would get her some extra money at a higher rate?*

She decided she would wait and make the decision based on the results of the appraisal on the second property. Property B was approved with a different lender and had a different appraisal company inspecting this one. Unfortunately though, this report put her in an even worse situation.

Unbeknownst to us, Diane was operating this other property as one of her home care facilities....unlicensed. The report noted a wheel chair lift on her staircase and individual locks on each bedroom door. When I asked her about these findings, she advised that she was in the process of getting the licensing requirements finalized and hence the need for the refinance money. The good news was that this value came in at the figure she had told us. The bad news was that this application now had to go to commercial lending. She was charged higher rates and fees and had to delay her closing.

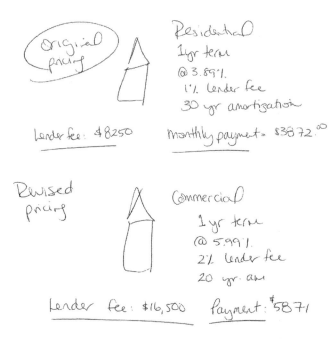

Original pricing

Residential
1 yr term
@ 3.89%
1% lender fee
30 yr amortization

Lender fee: $8250

monthly payment = $3872.00

Revised pricing

Commercial
1 yr term
@ 5.99%
2% lender fee
20 yr. am

Lender fee: $16,500

Payment: $5871

Figure S - Diane's 2nd property mortgage before & after

In the end, Diane ended up funding both applications, obtaining the licensing requirements and setting up a proper facility. It cost her more money than she budgeted for and a lot more time than she initially thought. The process created a domino effect of delays with her trades and eventual project completion. The #mortgagedont in this story is the delay of the appraisal and the obvious non-disclosure of the property's condition/use. It's the classic situation of what comes first - the chicken or the egg? Appraisals should be completed at the start of the application process but clients don't want to pay for them until they know they're approved with agreeable mortgage terms. By having the appraisal done up front, Diane would have spent $500 per property, had the correct approvals in place and the deals would have closed sooner. The waiting cost her an extra month and resulted in renovation delays. That inevitably translated into loss of business revenue as she wasn't licensed when originally planned.

Chapter 7

Dreaming of Your Renovations

Upgrading or building a home can be super exciting! You envision your new space with its updated materials and the fresh feel it'll bring to your home. Improvements can range from a simple coat of paint to a complete overhaul where you leave nothing of the old structure standing. Regardless of the amount of work that you'd like to get done, renovation financing has a few common pain points that are sure to cause frustration.

Although not its own 'C', renovation, or improvement financing, can fall into a couple of the existing categories. The obvious one is collateral. When you improve your property, you increase its value and make the home more marketable.

Clients will look for renovation financing at 3 different points:

1. Some begin the financing process before starting a project to ensure they have enough money to finish.

2. Others complete the renovations and then come to me to refinance their mortgage. They'd like to pay out the debt incurred while renovating. The payments are getting tough to manage and they're worried about their credit score. Or, they want to replenish the savings they used to fund this project. The property has a higher value and thus more room to pull out equity for a debt consolidation or top up of savings.

3. The worst case scenario occurs when an individual starts a renovation and runs out of money midway. In this case, the home owner is left scrambling to find funds to complete their project. Trades are probably calling. Fixtures are ready to get delivered upon payment, but the owner can't proceed any further because they didn't plan properly.

There are plenty of options to finance renovations and each person's situation will dictate the best solution. The problems that usually arise though aren't due the type of mortgage secured (lender, documents, conditions etc.). They're often caused by borrowers not taking the advice they're given which consists of 2 main recommendations:

1. Timing

I usually tell my clients to start the process a month before requiring money. Ideally, we complete their renovation financing two weeks before they actually need the money. This means we have the file approved, signed up and instructed at the lawyer with a closing date coming up two weeks later. It's way easier for me to move up a closing by a couple of days on a complete file than it is for me to complete an entire file within a couple of days. When renovating, payment schedules are usually set between you and your contractor/builder. We understand that being late on payment can impact the progress of your project. Help us help you by not leaving your mortgage request to the day before your contractor is waiting for payment.

2. Take all the money you can get

When you come in for a renovation mortgage and request for example, $250,000, I'll try and get you $350,000. If approved for this larger amount, take it. It's so much easier reducing a mortgage amount (or not taking that last advance on your construction draw), than scrambling to find more money because you went over budget.

Approximately 97% of my renovating clients insisted that they only get approved for what their builder quoted in their initial budget. As they approached the end of their projects, they ALL ran out of money. Some had to cash in savings, retirement plans or ask parents for help. Others had to run out and get approved for unsecured lines of credit or credit cards with double digits interest rates. In the end all their projects got finished and each one of them said "I wish I had listened and taken that extra money".

Although these solutions are simple in nature, you'd be shocked how many home owners cause unnecessary stress and anxiety in their lives while trying to manage a renovation project. With some well thought out planning, the financing aspect of your build can help you get finished quicker so you can enjoy that dream kitchen you've been fantasizing about.

Chapter 8

Mission.......Accomplished?

Purchasers. You've gone through each step of the application process with supreme diligence. When I asked for 2 paystubs, you gave me 5, just in case. Your downpayment accounts look like a map to the lost city of Atlantis. All transactions itemized and flow of funds pointing indisputably from one source account to another. It's crystal clear that not only did you save up all the money for this downpayment, but you have more than enough to accomplish what you're setting out to do. Your credit score is stellar and the best part in all of this is: you've sent it all to me during the pre-approval phase and I've reviewed it.

Property owners. You too, have dug up your property tax bills and annual mortgage statements from the dark and dingy basement storage room. You've connected me to your accountant and given us authorization to exchange information in order for me to better understand your business operation and self-employed income. Appraisal has been done and all figures have been agreed upon.

You can accomplish paying off all your debt and freeing up some monthly cash flow to grow your business.

The applications are inputted, reviewed and submitted for approval to the lenders and then we wait.....

Some lenders take a day to respond and others can take up to a week or more. It all depends on the mortgage product we're applying for and how popular or in demand it is at that given moment. With some files, I shop for best rate. For others, I need a more niche product. Your situation, your story, dictates the lender we approach. By this point, not only have we discussed the pros and cons of each eligible product, but we've also clarified why your mortgage is perfect for you.

While you wait, I'm communicating with the lender. I'm answering all their questions with confidence because I have your documentation on hand and can clarify any uncertainty. With some lenders, I can also satisfy conditions by submitting your paperwork up front which means less work for us to do leading up to the closing date. Once the lender is satisfied with your application and ensured that you fit within their lending guidelines, they send me an email with your commitment letter and I get to tell you: "Congratulations!! You're approved!!"

What follows then, is a flurry of activity:

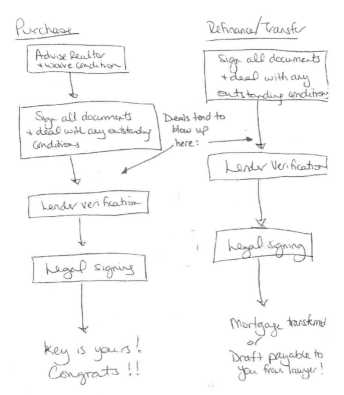

Figure T - Post-approval process

For a purchase, the closing date is more concrete and firm since it's a contract that is adhered to by two parties. Refinances on the other hand, tend to close quicker because you already own the home. The timing is entirely dependent on your ability to satisfy all the conditions and get your lawyer to complete the transaction. This makes the closing date more flexible. If any unforeseen circumstances arise, we're able to adjust the completion date and deal with the issues. We sometimes don't have this option with purchase closing dates.

Roxanne was so excited to move into her new house. When the mortgage was approved, she reviewed her commitment letter and the conditions. She immediately booked an appointment to come in and see me within a few days. We sat down, discussed her questions and she eagerly signed everything with her 'good luck' pen. We went over all the details of the remaining items and she nodded saying "this process was soooo easy and transparent".

She left my office with her homework note which included sending me a most recent bank account statement. Roxanne was expecting a bonus payment to come in over the next couple of weeks that she intended to use for the remainder of her downpayment. She promised to send it the moment the funds hit her account. I had diarized a reminder as well. Once the funds were in her account, we would still have 2 weeks before her closing date. Plenty of time to get this verified by the lender and off to her lawyer.

Roxanne, however, forgot to mention that she was the maid of honour at her best friend's wedding the weekend before her closing date. While she was preparing for bachelorette parties and helping her bestie finalize wedding plans, the need to send over a bank account statement fell lower on the to-do list. We get it. Life happens and it's way more exciting than chasing paperwork. Two weeks after our meeting I followed up with her. She emailed back right away confirming that the funds were indeed in her account and that I would have the statement the next morning. Another email two days later followed up with a phone call and Roxanne was still promising that she would send in that one missing piece of paper. She was so busy that was impossible for her to send it over before the wedding. The missing piece of paper finally came in 3 days prior to funding.

The domino effect was clear:

- The lawyer was hounding Roxanne and I for their instructions because we were now at risk of not closing on time. Roxanne would be charged extension fees from the seller of the house she was buying;

- The lender wasn't sending over any instructions until they had a completely verified file. They were getting upset with me for not providing the missing segment of this file;

- I had no document to submit. Roxanne was getting anxious fielding all the phone calls and messages from her lawyer, realtor and my team. We were all voicing concerns and hinting at extra costs......all of which could have been avoided.

The good news in this specific case, was that the file was fairly straight forward and easy to verify. Income was confirmed in the first attempt and the downpayment was all in her savings. Her bonus was confirmed by her paystub, and there was no appraisal required because Roxanne was a high ratio purchase (10% downpayment). The lawyer got documents the day before closing and with his experienced team, closed the deal the morning after the originally scheduled closing date. Her only costs were a night at a hotel while her stuff remained in a moving truck. By noon the next day, with keys in her hand, she was happily unloading boxes into her new home.

Refinance applicants; you don't get keys to a new home. You either get a whole bunch of debt paid off and a huge weight lifted off your shoulders, or a draft made out to your name once your lawyer closes your deal. This marks the beginning of your new chapter as you take steps towards the next dream you want to realize. All thanks to the equity you built up in your home over the years.

As a TEAM, you, your realtor, your lawyer and I went from analyzing three significant aspects of your lifestyle to locating the best property for you or taking out the right amount of equity to help you reach your financial goals. Your file was submitted for review. You got approved and signed a lot of documents. The appraisal and verification steps were completed and the instructions got to your lawyer. You signed more paperwork with your lawyer and now, you're the proud owner of a new home. Or you're the recipient of a cheque from your lawyer (for the equity you took out to pay your bills or purchase that investment property with). Although going through it seemed endless, there really were a lot people involved in getting you to the finish line.

Overall, the main take-away and theme of this book, is disclosure. The more you tell us, show us, and provide to us, the better off we'll all be. We prefer having more information rather than scrambling to find it last minute. It's so much easier to deal with confirmed data upfront and navigate through its challenges. Having to work around roadblocks when you don't have the complete story and time is ticking against you is highly stressful. Although your friend/co-worker/family member's mortgage seems like it may have been easier, just remember that their experience was based on their story. Not yours. Moreover, just because you may have 60% equity in your home and you need a tiny little mortgage in comparison to the value of your property, doesn't mean that you get to by-pass all the other factors that determine your credit worthiness. We only ask for the information we need.

Our goal is to get you home, or your debt paid out, or free up your equity so you can pay for son's first year university. Good news: he got into an amazing program at a US school!! Bad news: he got into an amazing program at a US school with no international scholarships. By allowing me into your world, I get to understand your story so I can present it to the lender with the best solution for you. This story comes from our conversations and your documents. You have all the pieces I need to create a solution tailored to your needs. No, mortgages aren't complicated. They just need the patience and vision to draw out the right story.

And finally, there's a 6th and final C which we haven't discussed yet: common sense. Although mortgage financing is all about guidelines, policies and calculations, there is room for us to apply common sense and ask for exceptions when they're warranted. I hope that by simplifying a seemingly complex process and showing you that a mortgage is really like piecing together your puzzle, the anxiety that the word 'mortgage' produces, will be gone. A mortgage is a tool that when used properly, helps you build wealth and achieve your financial goals.

You've Got Questions?

1. Why should I use a mortgage broker/agent?

There are many reasons to use a mortgage broker/agent but here are the top 3:

A) We work for you. We tend to be self-employed which means we only get paid if we fund your transaction and to fund your transaction, we have to keep you happy. Any successful business owner will tell you that to close a sale, you have to provide a product or service that's in demand, have the best service and competitive pricing. We target the best rate and terms for your financing needs and our goal is a flawless customer experience.

B) We're licensed by a governing body. The Financial Services Commission of Ontario (FSCO), regulates the mortgage brokering industry by licensing mortgage brokers, agents, brokerages and administrators. Licensed mortgage professionals are constantly updating their skills with mandatory continuing education courses and have to meet experience and suitability requirements. Rest assured that we're always up to date on lender policies and government industry changes.

C) We have access to many different lenders. By not working for one institution and trying to fit you into one box, I can shop around with all the lenders you see on the street, and many you don't. You're not a candidate for one lender? That doesn't mean we can't find you a competitive mortgage with another. Having many different lender options also means that we have access to all kinds of rate specials and promos that we pass along to you.

2. Aren't mortgage brokers used by those who can't get approved by the banks?

Absolutely not!

We can put together all types of mortgages. In fact, I deal with many 'A' lenders for our top scoring borrowers. Did you know there are lenders with fantastic rates and terms that are only accessible through a mortgage agent/broker? By being partners with these lenders, we can provide additional competitive mortgage options. These lenders look for qualified borrowers from broker partners in good standing with them.

Credit unions and trust companies also provide options for competitive pricing. And for the applicants who don't fit the traditional bank models? We have access to alternate lenders who have created niche products specializing in harder to place mortgages (i.e. for self-employed borrowers with non-traditional income types).

3. My credit isn't good and I know I won't get approved. Why should I bother applying?

Because some lenders know that life happens. You may have had some credit blips – a few late payments, maybe even some collections. Wouldn't you want to learn how to repair it and plan to buy your own place? Sometimes, what you think is bad i.e. a large balance on a credit card that haunts you in your sleep, may not be an actual bad credit scoring for an application. Let me take a look and advise. If in fact your score is affected and doesn't meet the minimum required by the main banks, no worries. We have alternate lenders we can approach for short term solutions until your score increases.

4. I don't make a salary. What kind of paperwork will I need to provide?

This is covered in detail in chapter 3.

5. Why do the lenders ask for so much paperwork?

The concise answer for this is risk analysis and data integrity. They want to make sure you'll pay them back so they have to verify the information on the application to ensure its accuracy.

6. I want to buy a place with some rental income (i.e. basement or separate unit in the same house). Can I use that income to help me qualify?

If the unit is a basement and it is legal and retrofitted, yes you can use a part of the rent with all lenders. If it's not though, then we deal with lenders who don't have this zoning requirement.

If you're looking at a multi-unit property i.e. duplex, triplex and fourplex, yes, we can use a portion of the rental income to help you qualify.

This topic is also covered in more detail in chapter 6.

7. Why do you use the term A and B lending?

"A" lending refers to the most competitive priced mortgages and is reserved for "A" clients – the ones that fit into most lenders' boxes. These clients tend to be strong in all 5C's of credit.

Alternate lending, sometimes referred to as "B" lending, involves more risk. This is usually either in the form of bruised credit or non-traditional income. This risk prevents you getting approved at the 'A' lenders so rates and fees are higher.

For borrowers who don't fit in either A or B lending, there are private lending solutions which have the highest rates and fees. These clients present the most challenging situations and are provided with short term mortgages to address their shortfalls. Once the issues resolve, we work to get them back into A or B lenders.

8. Can I refer my friends to you?

Of course you can and we hope you do!

Summary of #MortgageDonts

General #MortgageDonts:

- Don't follow the crowd and think that all mortgages are the same. Just because your friend got one type of mortgage, doesn't mean that this is the best option for you.

Income #MortgageDonts:

- Don't change/quit/get laid off of employment and not advise your agent/broker in the midst of your transaction.

- Don't be vague or dismissive of details regarding your pay. More is more in this case. Give us as much information as possible.

<u>Downpayment #MortgageDonts:</u>

- Don't forget to tell me the details. Although you may think it's insignificant or not an impact to your mortgage, tell me anyway. I especially need to know about the one off transactions in your account or movement of large amounts of money.

<u>Credit #MortgageDonts:</u>

- Don't wait to pay off more than the minimum payment AFTER the due date. Make the minimum required on time. Then make any additional payments after if your intent is to make a larger payment.

- Don't commit to more debt during the approval process. Lenders reserve the right to pull a new credit bureau 30 days prior to your closing date to ensure that you're still credit worthy and qualify.

- Don't ignore incorrect information on your credit report. It could impact your ability to get approved at a later date by reducing your score. Inaccurate information should be rectified. Sign up for online credit alerts with your credit bureau provider to prevent identity theft and fraud along with erroneous reporting of debt.

Property #MortgageDonts:

- Don't forget to disclose all the properties you own and their actual expenses and incomes (if any). Omitting information will just prolong the process and make it frustrating for all parties involved. Mortgages are now reported on credit bureaus and most lenders and mortgage brokers perform searches to cross reference information for accuracy. The more accurate details you give me up front, the more streamline the process becomes and the faster we get your funds you to.

- Don't assume a value on your property. It's worth the few hundred dollars to get an appraisal and plan out your financing with real numbers as opposed to going through the process twice - with assumed figures and then with readjusted, accurate numbers.

- Don't omit anything about the property. Tell me about the good, the bad, and the ugly. If your roof blew off in the last storm, it's ok. Tell me so we can manage your file properly. We don't want the appraiser noting defects on your report. This would risk having your file cancelled by the lender or paying for another appraisal once your roof is finished to confirm the house is at 100% complete.

Construction/Renovation #MortgageDonts:

- Don't wait until you need the money to request financing. Get started early.

Don't turn down a larger approved mortgage amount. Take it! Depending on the type of mortgage you're arranging, you can always reduce it if you don't use the entire amount.

Document Preparation Checklists

Purchase:

- Mortgage application with your personal information

- Income documents based on your employment structure (detailed in chapter 3)

- Purchase agreement

- Listing – if the purchase was a private deal, advise the mortgage professional how you learned about this sale

- Downpayment confirmation – 3 months account statements. If any portion is gifted or borrowed from a line of credit, advise the mortgage professional for further guidance

- Lawyer contact information

- Void cheque for the account you want to make your payments out of

- 2 pieces of ID

- If you own any other property

    o Mortgage statement

    o Property tax bill

    o Proof of condo fees (if applicable)

    o Lease (if applicable)

- If you're separated/divorced you'll need to send in a copy of your separation agreement

- Bankruptcy documents (if applicable)

Refinance/Transfer:

- Mortgage application with your personal information

- Income documents based on your employment structure (detailed in chapter 3)

- Mortgage statement of the property we're refinancing/transferring

- Property tax bill of the property we're refinancing/transferring

- Lawyer contact information

- Void cheque for the account you want to make your payments out of

- 2 pieces of ID

- If you own any other property

    o Mortgage statement

    o Property tax bill

    o Proof of condo fees (if applicable)

    o Lease (if applicable)

- If you're separated/divorced you'll need to send in a copy of your separation agreement

- Bankruptcy documents (if applicable)

7 Questions You Must Ask a Mortgage Professional Before Working with Them

1. What documents do you need up front?

After reading this book, you now know that the answer they should be giving you is 'all your documents'. They can send you a list of items they want based on your conversation or tell you in person/over the phone. You don't want to work with someone who won't take the time to review your paperwork upfront. Any miscommunication or misunderstanding will happen during this phase so make sure you work with someone who wants your paperwork sooner than later.

2. What is your timeline for service?

A mortgage professional has service levels for each part of the application process. Review and feedback of the initial application takes x amount of time. Submitting for approval takes y amount of time. Review of final conditions to get to funding takes z amount of time. Although unforeseen circumstances arise, the mortgage agent should be able to give you an idea of how long each part will take.

3. When, and how, will you tell me my mortgage approval details?

Some brokers prefer to meet you in person to discuss approval details. Others are comfortable sending your rate, mortgage amount and monthly payment over email. Choose the communication method you prefer. If you want a phone call rather than an email, let them know.

4. Do I have any input on the lender you approach for my file?

If your only concern is pricing, then the broker will send your file to the best priced lender available for you. If you want some say in the mortgage options (pre-payment privileges, equity line of credit), then let the mortgage pro know. These details can dictate the lender so it's important for the broker to know prior to submitting your file for approval.

5. Who will be handling my file?

Many mortgage professionals work in teams to provide the best customer experience. Getting introduced to other members on the team would be beneficial. You now have more people to communicate with and won't be surprised when a third party asks you for sensitive documents.

6. What's your plan B?

Sometimes, applications don't go as planned. You don't want to hear 'sorry, we can't help you at this time'. This would leave you back at square one, with less time to arrange your financing, so your mortgage professional should have a backup plan. Ideally one they can initiate themselves or refer you to a trusted partner who can take over quickly.

7. What is your fee for your services or how do you get paid?

Mortgage professionals vary in the way they get paid depending on who they work for and the complexity of the file. Sometimes, mortgage agents/brokers charge fees on files that are more complicated and involve alternate lending solutions. Fees should be fully disclosed up front with your mortgage approval details so you decide on whether to proceed.

About the Author

Athena was born and raised in Toronto, Ontario by immigrant parents. She earned a Bachelor of Science (Hons) degree from the University of Toronto. While in university, she worked part time for a real estate company focused on new condo development sites. It through this job that she learned about the world of mortgages.

After she graduated, she worked for a large Canadian bank as a mortgage specialist for ten years. In year eleven, she realized that her client base was expanding and needed different options so she got licensed as a mortgage agent. She co-founded Sherwood Mortgage Group with Anthony Contento and started with a team of nine agents in December 2008. Ten years later, Sherwood Mortgage Group operates in two provinces with over fifty mortgage professionals.

In February 2018, as a response to industry changes and market demands, Athena and her business partner Anthony, launched Sherwood Capital Mortgage Investment Corporation (MIC). The MIC provides investment and lending options in the alternate lending space.

She's received numerous awards throughout her career. Athena was most recently recognized as a Woman of Influence by her industry peers. When she's not negotiating mortgages for her clients, Athena volunteers at a women's shelter as a tutor. Hot yoga is her go-to stress reliever and she tries to travel to one new destination each year with her family.

She's a sucker for french fries and lives in Toronto with her two teenage boys and her enormous five pound yorkie named George.

You can connect with Athena at
athenaconstantinou.ca
or follow her on twitter @somanyhatsforme

42901590R00086

Made in the USA
Middletown, DE
18 April 2019